Understanding Harper Lee's To Kil

- **A complete GCSE Study Guide for Summer 2015 & 2016 Exams.**

By Gavin Smithers

Another one of **Gavin's Guides** – study books packed with insight. They aim to help you raise your grade!

Understanding Harper Lee's "To Kill a Mockingbird" is a complete study guide, written especially for students and teachers who are preparing for GCSE in Summer 2015 and 2016.

Series Editor: Gill Chilton

The complete text of To Kill a Mockingbird (Arrow) is widely available, including on Amazon. You will need a copy of this text, in paperback or as an e-book, to use alongside this Study Guide.

Contents

Let's Get Started

Harper Lee's "To Kill a Mockingbird" has been a favourite GCSE text for many years. It's easy to see why; it asks questions about social equality and fairness, which are always relevant. It explores how the world looks, to adults and to children. Through the innocent eyes of Scout and Jem, prejudice and hypocrisy are as clear as they are groundless.

It is full of evocative description and sharp characterisation, and there is plenty of dramatic tension in the second half of the novel. Reading it makes us temporary residents in Maycomb, a small town in the deep south of America. We have to ask ourselves how many of the unpleasant attitudes which pass for normal among most of that community are attitudes we have absorbed too.

If you've bought this guide because "To Kill a Mockingbird" is included in what you have to study for GCSE, then, in my opinion, you've just taken another step towards doing well in your exam. Regardless of which exam board your school enters you for, you will have to answer one question on the novel. You will have 45-60 minutes for this; you may be able to take an unmarked copy of the text into the exam with you, for quick reference.

Edexcel tend to ask a question about a particular character, or a theme. Other exam boards may subdivide their question, to include analysing the content and method of a short printed extract, and relating it to the novel as a whole, and then ask you to write more extensively about another episode or a different theme.

All examiners are looking for the same elements in your answer-evidence that you understand the plot and characters, and that you understand what you feel as you read it, and how and why these feelings come about. This guide addresses all of those aspects of the novel, as well as the historical background.

Understanding that context helps us to see very clearly what Harper Lee intends the message or meaning of her story to be.

Overall, about 75% of candidates will achieve grades A-C in English Literature GCSEs, with Bs and Cs the commonest result. **My aim in writing this guide is to lead you towards the upper range of grades, by helping you to achieve a thorough understanding of the novel**, and giving you practical advice on how to manage your time in the exam and how to write a really effective exam essay.

So,why a Gavin's Guide? It is likely you have browsed online or gone to a bookshop, and found that there are several study guides on this text already. Many of them are useful for summarising the plot and the characters.

Few, if any, explain the context of the novel as thoroughly as this one, or concentrate so much on how Harper Lee manages and organises our response as we read.

And understanding these aspects of the purpose of the novel- and showing your examiner that you do- will make it easier for you to achieve a higher grade.

I am a private tutor in Broadway, Worcestershire, and this book was written initially for my own English Literature students. I wrote it to help them achieve a better grade, and appreciate what this principled, determined writer wanted to say. Whether you have chosen the paperback or the e-book, I hope it will help you too.

What this short guide can do

This guide will help you to understand clearly what Harper Lee wanted to say when she wrote "To Kill a Mockingbird"- and where that motivation came from.

It will also help you to improve your essay technique.

For GCSE, it is no longer enough to know what happens in a novel. You need to look at the "why" and "how" of the way in which the writer has created the text. That includes being able to relate events which take place many chapters apart; I highlight those connections for you.

So, to deepen your understanding, all you need is a few clear hours….and the willingness to begin with an open, curious mind.

This short interpretative guide is intended as a supplement to, not a substitute for, your lessons at school. It also comes with a big warning-

……………*this guide will tell you what happens in the novel, almost from the start.*

I make no apologies for "plot spoiling". It is quite deliberate- because a study guide is useful after you have read the novel for yourself, all the way through. It is not a short cut that means you don't have to read the novel!

Again, after- and only after- you have read the novel for yourself, you may be interested in seeing adaptations on film or in the theatre. Like other GCSE texts, a stage version of this novel may be appearing in a theatre near you- check your local listings, and see whether a school trip is planned, or possible.

But bear in mind the fact that a stage production, lasting perhaps two hours, cannot hope to transfer the whole of the novel. It does not have enough time, so it will be a selective and partial representation, with much material left out, including important elements of the story. A theatre cast will also be much smaller in number than the roll call of characters in the novel.

The same is true of the distinguished and powerful 1962 film of the book, starring Gregory Peck. I analyse the film version later in this guide. Seeing it is useful in the sense that it will prompt you to ask why the director chose to include what he did, and excluded what he did; you will spot a few small discrepancies.

So multimedia versions of the novel can heighten your awareness of the issue of artistic control, and how it shapes the novel, the play and the film in different ways. Watching the film and seeing the play will not, by itself, improve your essays or your understanding of the novel. For that, you need to read on…..

You can email me- at grnsmithers@hotmail.co.uk- if you feel there is something that you still don't understand. I hope to help you further, or point you to further useful resources.

My love of literature began when I studied for an English degree at Oxford University. Today, unravelling and appreciating language remains a lifelong passion. If this little book can move you towards that too. Then it will be doubly worthwhile!

How this novel is structured

This novel, first published in 1960, won the **Pulitzer Prize** in 1961. More than **40 million copies** of it have been sold. It is almost impossible to find anyone who has read it and does not have fond memories of it. **A famous film version** was made in 1962 (Gregory Peck won an Oscar for his portrayal of Atticus Finch).

Intriguingly, publication is now due in July 2015 of the novel to which this one is a prequel. It is to be called "Go Set a Watchman", and will explore Scout's relationship with the world, and her father, in the 1950s. This is not a new novel, but the original version, from which the idea of narrating a novel about Scout's childhood, and from her point of view, emerged.

"To Kill a Mockingbird" is in two parts. Part One has 11 chapters. Part Two takes up chapters 12 to 31, and makes up 60% of the story.

Why **two parts**? The first brings Scout's childhood vividly to life; it is as if we are sitting on the veranda, or in the treehouse, and observing the **attitudes** of the people of Maycomb. We adjust to their frequent **prejudices**, their habitual lack of flexibility, and we see them for the limited people they are.

Our view, as readers, is rather like the intelligent but self-effacing Atticus's- he disagrees with many of their attitudes, but he has lived amid these people all his life, and so he respects their right to hold the views they do. It is his purpose to protect them against their own **stupidity**. Both as a parent and as a lawyer, Atticus cannot prevent people from making mistakes which get them into trouble, but he can and does try to ensure that **lessons are learnt**. The evil men do does not make them inherently evil by nature; Atticus sees bad behaviour and prejudice as an affliction of the community as a whole- **"Maycomb's usual disease"**.

His **overriding tolerance** for the mistakes (and foolishness) of others expresses itself in an attitude of **non-violent protest** (the approach which eventually started to win the battles for civil rights and against racial segregation in the USA).

Just as Atticus insists that his children should, as it were, get **inside the skin of other people**, to see the world as they see it,

Harper Lee gives us the time and space, in Part One, to see the world of Maycomb as its own residents do, before- in Part Two- she dramatises the trial of Tom Robinson.

Historical context

If you have studied JB Priestley's play "An Inspector Calls", you will notice a similarity; that play was first seen in England in 1946, but it is set, very specifically, in 1912. Why? Because Priestley wants to set out two divergent routes which Britain in 1946 can take (on its journey to decide on the structure and values of post-War society). The 1912 setting helps him to show how deep-rooted and hard to change some people's attitudes are, and it helps him to dramatise what is at stake *now*, for the audience of his own time, in 1946.

"To Kill a Mockingbird" was first **published in 1960**, but its **story starts in 1933**. This is partly because it reflects Harper Lee's own childhood. Similarly, Charlotte Bronte's novel "Jane Eyre" builds a highly dramatic story, after an extended history of Jane's childhood and education which is strongly autobiographical.

The setting- in rural Alabama- helps Harper Lee to **dramatise racial prejudice** as an everyday, accepted but cancerous attitude. Atticus calls it "Maycomb's usual disease", at the end of Chapter 9. Alabama is at the heart of the old slave trade, so its citizens are **conditioned (by their history) to assume that being white means being innately superior**.

The novel **criticises** and **ridicules** this prejudice ruthlessly-particularly as it presents itself in the character of Atticus' sister, Alexandra- and the court scene lays it to rest, once and for all, **as a lie**. But Maycomb and its people have a symbolic value. They stand for the prejudices and **small-town, inbred thinking** which is endemic in all parts of America, and is **still as current in 1960 (when the book was published) as it was in the Alabama of 1933 (when it was set).**

In 2007, Harper Lee received the **Presidential Medal of Freedom** from George W Bush. It is not a literary award, but it recognises outstanding contributions to the national interests of the United States, to world peace or to culture. The award serves as a judgment that, by raising the issues of multicultural human rights at the time it did, the novel **accelerated peace and progress**, and that Harper Lee's tale is not just about a small southern town with a made-up name; it is of real national and international significance. In **refusing to accept the principle of racism**, while giving us an insight into where and how it arises, and how hard it is to change, it confronts some deeply entrenched fears and social problems.

While we find it very hard to understand how societies could be run on the basis of racial segregation, the history of the USA shows us that the abolition of slavery in 1865 did not put an end to discrimination. It took another 100 years for American society to become equal, even simply in the legal sense. And, just when the beginning of the end of racial discrimination dawned in America, the first protests against apartheid in South Africa were only about to start, at the end of the 1960s. The same battles had yet to be fought in another part of the world.

One of the great achievements of "To Kill a Mockingbird" is its success in presenting the mass of **ordinary white American**

citizens (apart from the Ewells, who are "trash") **as basically decent people who are also racist**.

We have had the same discussions in Britain in the last twenty years about "institutional racism", in the police and other public institutions. **Atticus and Judge Taylor** are based on real people, but their values and morality are polished for us. They **are good men**, who **resist the overwhelming culture of racism among their "friends" and fellow citizens**. The fact that the jury has to think before it condemns Tom Robinson is a small step in the right direction, and a victory of sorts, because it paves the way for a pattern of questioning, challenging and eventually changing the status quo. When we understand how deeply entrenched racism was, in 20th century America, and for how long it went unquestioned, we can see how brave Atticus is- and why he knows from the moment he accepts the case that his defence of Tom Robinson will be futile.

In Chapter 1, we read that Atticus' office has very little in it, but one of those items is **the Code of Alabama**- the state constitution. It is "unsullied"- not thumbed through or much used- because **the impartiality of the law is one thing, and the custom of local courts quite another**. This is why Atticus tells Jem, in Chapter 23, that reducing the risk of miscarriages of justice, by reserving the right to pass a death sentence to a judge (rather than a jury) will take 50 or 60 years. Changing the law, to make it fair, is almost impossible; and then applying those changes is just as difficult. It was the federal (national) government of the USA which eventually had to force the state of Alabama to change its discriminatory local laws, in the 1950s.

The Scottsboro Boys' trials – an important source

The trial which forms the dramatic focus of the novel is influenced by the case of the Scottsboro Boys. They were nine black teenagers who were accused, in Alabama, of raping two white girls on a train in 1931. Aspects of the subsequent series of trials went to the heart of the legal system and of **the principle of a fair trial**- the exact focus of Atticus' closing remarks to the jury in Chapter 20.

The fact that the **juries** in the trials of the Scottsboro Boys **were composed only of white men** became an important constitutional point, because it provided grounds for appeal to higher courts when the (prejudiced) local juries returned guilty verdicts.

The Alabama Supreme Court upheld seven of the convictions, even though- as well as doubts over the evidence given for the prosecution- there were concerns about whether the jury and the trial were unbiased; about the quality of the legal defence; and about the severity of the sentences (indiscriminate death penalties, regardless of the fact that all of the accused could not have been equally at fault).

In a retrial in Alabama, **the prosecution evidence fell apart but the jury still found the defendants guilty**- precisely the outcome in the novel, where Harper Lee uses Jem's reactions to highlight the absurdity of the verdict. The judge in the Scottsboro case overruled the verdict and ordered another trial. Judge Taylor does not do this- instead, Tom Robinson's case will go to an appeal, which is the same as the first part of the process outlined above- an appeal to the Alabama Supreme Court.

The new trial of the Scottsboro Boys featured a jury with one black juror, and a biased judge. Its "guilty" verdicts led to an appeal to the US Supreme Court, which found that the jury was unconstitutional because of its overwhelming white bias- which refers us back to the Alabama constitution of 1901. **Atticus knows that** for cultural reasons **an all-white jury will find Tom guilty even though he can show the "evidence" is a pack of lies**. An Alabama jury will always accept the word of a white accuser; Atticus discusses this with his brother in Chapter 9, so that **the reader is prepared from a very early stage for a miscarriage of justice in Chapter 21.**

The dramatic episode with the **lynch gang** in Chapter 15 **reflects the fact of extreme racial intolerance**, and the blatant desire to **deny justice to African Americans**. Before the first trial, the jail in Scottsboro was besieged by such a mob, but the sheriff resisted them; in the novel, **the role of standing up against the mob naturally goes to Atticus**. The real trial was witnessed by a white-only public gallery (who had to have permits for admittance, because of the graphic nature of the accusations). By making Tom Robinson's trial open to attendance by all races, and having the children sit in "the coloured balcony", Lee can motivate Bob Ewell's vengeance.

More importantly, though, she can present **the perversion of justice through the children's eyes**, and let us see Atticus in action, providing the type of conscientious defence the Scottsboro boys were denied in their initial trials. Bob and Mayella Ewell, and their solicitor, Horace Gilmer, are **shamelessly racist** in their behaviour in a mixed-race courtroom. The reader is with the children, in the seats saved for us by the Rev Sykes; it is clear where our sympathies lie. Harper Lee would be less able to guide our judgment if she had simply copied the facts of the Scottsboro trials, and had a white-only public gallery. She takes various details of the Scottsboro case and **adapts them, for dramatic effect**.

In Chapter 23, Atticus reveals that one of the jury wanted to acquit Tom, but that racist cultural norms meant that he could not persuade the others. At the end of Chapter 21, the death sentence is not mentioned; no sentence is passed. It is only in Chapter 23 that Atticus tells Scout that, if his appeal fails, or if he is refused a new trial (on the grounds of a perverse verdict) Tom will be executed by electric chair, unless the Governor of Alabama commutes his sentence.

The historical norm was for a death sentence where a black defendant was convicted of raping a white woman. One of the Scottsboro Boys, Clarence Norris, had his death sentence reduced to life in prison, by the Governor of Alabama, in 1938. Atticus' reading of what may happen to Tom- that he will not necessarily be executed because of the miscarriage of justice- is accurate. Tom could be saved on appeal, and he **is harmless, but he is shot- like a mockingbird- as he tries to take flight over the prison wall.**

It is interesting that Tom's appeal is not on the grounds that the jury should not have been all-white; that is a legal point which would only come into play when a further appeal goes to the Supreme Court, an option which Tom's shooting in prison makes impossible. Atticus can obtain an appeal for Tom on the more dramatic grounds that this jury ignored the evidence because it was **so biased that it could not provide a fair trial.**

Both Mr Gilmer's calculated rudeness to Tom in Chapter 19 and Mayella's eventual refusal to answer any questions in Chapter 18 reflect aspects of the reports of the Scottsboro trial in Decatur, Alabama (a small town much like Maycomb). In the real case, there was a Dr Lynch, who knew that the two women had not been raped; years after the case, he conceded that he could have given evidence for the defence, but that doing so would have destroyed his medical practice and his livelihood. Atticus alludes to this sort of **social pressure** in Chapter 23, when he explains that people who make their living in the community (like the shopkeeper Mr Link Deas) excuse themselves from jury service because they do not have the courage to make contentious decisions which may alienate some of their customers.

Atticus says that the courtroom should give the accused "a square deal"; the Scottsboro retrial defence lawyer at Decatur (Leibowitz) used the term "a square shake of the dice". Although one of the women accusers arrived belatedly (very much in the manner of Calpurnia at the start of Chapter 21), and then went on to admit that the prosecution case was untrue, and motivated by selfishness and a disregard for black people, the jury still found the defendants guilty. But it came to this verdict overnight, after deliberating for eleven hours; the foreman of the jury had held out for life sentences, not execution- which was as good as saying that the defendants were not guilty.

Lee uses the device of **delaying the speed of the verdict** as a triumph for Atticus, and a sign that **the dam of racial prejudice has developed its first crack** (see Chapter 23). She does not defer the verdict till the next day, because that would sacrifice dramatic tension. In Tom Robinson's trial, it is almost 4pm at the end of Chapter19, and the guilty verdict is delivered, at the end of Chapter 21, some time after 11pm- as late as possible, but still on the same day.

We can see the ways in which the Scottsboro Boys' case offered Harper Lee a great deal of **dramatic** potential, which she **heightens**, for example, by having just **one defendant** (instead of nine) and **one accuser**, instead of two. The years of the Decatur trials, 1933-37, put the fictional Tom Robinson case (1935) at the heart of the same time frame. Readers from 1960 onwards would be used to the- now settled- view that the Scottsboro trials had exposed the depth of prejudice in the southern states, and in

Alabama in particular. **Maycomb** therefore has a symbolic significance much greater than itself. It **has its own dump**, but perhaps **it is, itself a dump of racial prejudice** in the wider landscape of America as a whole.

The novel confronts and dramatises the jury's inability to judge the case on the merits of the evidence; this outrages Jem, and Atticus describes it as "Maycomb's usual disease". If you read the history of the Scottsboro Boys trials, your overwhelming sense is that, while some judges and juries disregarded the evidence, the reasons for the retrials were more to do with faults in the legal constitution (the way juries were selected). **Harper Lee wishes to interrogate and cross-examine** not the framework of the courts but **the deep prejudices of the people of Maycomb**, both individually (Mrs Dubose, Mr Underwood, Bob Ewell, Aunt Alexandra) and as a community.

Atticus defends Tom Robinson, and the white community in Maycomb disapproves (Francis Hancock and Mrs Dubose are not alone in labelling him a "nigger-lover") but he is still re-elected, unopposed, to the Alabama State Legislature. Why?

The American Civil War (1861-1865) had been fought between the Union of 23 northern states and some others, against the Confederate States. The underlying issues were political and economic; the common interests of the Confederate States were farming and slave-owning. Slavery was abolished and slaves in Alabama were freed in 1865. The population of Alabama at that time was just under 1 million, of whom almost half were slaves.

After the War, states like Alabama retained a high measure of control over their own laws and government. **Abolishing slavery did not begin to address the issue of racial segregation, which Alabama did much to maintain well into the 1960s.** The Alabama Constitution, in the form we are interested in, originated in 1901. It is very long (310000 words). As Alabama became less rural and agricultural, and more industrial, its laws were slow to adjust.

The 1901 constitution excluded most African Americans and most poor white people from voting in elections, by making registering to vote depend on paying taxes and a literacy test. Some 181000 African Americans had been eligible to vote in 1900, but by 1903 that number had fallen to less than 3000. It made schools racially segregated (there are only white children at the school in Maycomb) and it made interracial marriage illegal. The schoolteacher, Miss Gates, reveals **the white community's fears about interracial marriage** at the end of Chapter 26.

Racial segregation in Alabama actually became stricter as time went on, extending to prisons (1911), hospitals (1915), toilets, hotels and restaurants (1928) and bus stop waiting rooms (1945). Boo Radley's arrest at the age of 33 (in Chapter 1, when he stabbed his father in the leg with a pair of scissors) precedes prison segregation in 1911.

Alabama was at the heart of the national awareness of the segregation issue again at the end of 1955. The arrest of Rosa Parks for refusing to give up her seat on a bus to a white person in Montgomery- where Atticus qualified as a lawyer, and met his wife- led to a year-long campaign, at the end of which the US Supreme Court ruled that the laws in Montgomery and Alabama requiring segregated buses were unconstitutional. In March 1955, a 15 year old girl, Claudette Colvin, had been arrested for the same so-called offence. Martin Luther King (a Baptist, like Miss Maudie Atkinson) was one of the leaders of the boycott and his mantra of non-violent protest began to attract national attention from this point onwards.

After the Civil War, three amendments to the US constitution had abolished slavery, made African Americans US citizens, and given them (the men- women, of whatever race, were not entitled) the vote in elections. But between 1890 and 1908 the southern states passed new laws of their own to make voting registration almost impossible for African Americans, so that their interests were not represented at all. This was only addressed in the mid-1960s by new national civil rights legislation.

Once we understand **the historical significance of Alabama as a state where many of these defining and critical events took place**, we can see how Maycomb, the fictional town in the novel, symbolises the wider cultural prejudices which go well beyond Alabama into the rest of America and beyond.

Atticus Finch is a coherent and convincing character throughout "To Kill a Mockingbird", except in part of Chapter 23, where he is too obviously a moral mouthpiece. This is where **the meaning of the novel** is to be found, in its warning that **there will be a price, or bill, to pay for discrimination**, in all of its forms. His small victory- in keeping the jury out for more than just a few minutes, before it convicts Tom Robinson- proves that the racist reflex or impulse can be challenged, but that curing it, and putting a proper emphasis on fairness for everyone instead, will take many years.

The overview that you've just read explains **why Maycomb is** a symbolic place, and **the perfect setting for a tale of prejudice**.

You've seen, too, how Harper Lee borrowed facts from the real-life Scottsboro trials, and adapted them for the dramatic content of the courtroom scenes.

Both the nature of these adaptations, and the fact that they came from **a real miscarriage of justice, in a real rape case, where justice was denied, blatantly, to African American defendants** show that the issue at the heart of the novel is the issue of racial prejudice.

Next, we will look in more detail at the story of the novel, and at the methods Harper Lee uses in telling it.

Chapter by chapter breakdown of the book

Preface Quotation or "Epigraph"

The quotation attached to the opening page of the novel is from the English writer and critic Charles Lamb (1775-1834) - **"Lawyers, I suppose, were children once".**

Atticus is a lawyer. Jem seems to have an ambition to do the same as his father, although in moments of crisis (end of Chapter 5, end of Chapter 26, Chapter 23) his resolve crumbles, because he is idealistic, and not yet old enough to absorb the unfairness or disappointment of working through the flawed legal system.

Harper Lee and her sister Alice were also familiar with the law.

Atticus suggests (Chapter 16) that **a police force made up of children** would be able to defuse adult aggression and mob violence.

The thesis of the novel is that **the law needs to be applied with the clear-sighted fairness of a child's point of view**. If that were done, the outcome in court would always be fair.

And a word about the title

The title "To Kill a Mockingbird" refers to Atticus' saying, in chapter 10, that "it's a sin to kill a mockingbird". The ellipsis makes us think of the words left out; "it's a sin". At the end of chapter 30, Heck Tate says that "it's a sin" to put Boo Radley into the public limelight, and he repeats that idea- "that's a sin". Scout then makes the link even clearer, when she compares a public appearance for Boo with shooting a mockingbird.

The link is deliberate; Boo and Tom Robinson are both "mockingbirds", innocent targets of prejudice. Around both of them- because of Boo's stabbing his father and Tom's short prison term for fighting- hangs an undeserved reputation for violence. They are, in fact, harmless. Public attention would "kill" or destroy Boo in the same way racial prejudice killed Tom.

Chapter 1

The foundations for the dramatic court scenes much later are laid here. We start to fit together the first pieces of the large jigsaw of interconnections in Maycomb. It is an **insular, inward-looking** backwater. The people who live there are not very interested in the wider world, and they **resist change**. They have a strong sense of their own history and heritage. A mixture of in-breeding and genetic deficiencies means that there is no new blood- each generation of these old families lives and behaves **just like their ancestors**. Sometimes this can be amusing (Aunt Alexandra has a list of sayings about each family's characteristics in Chapter 13) but there is a serious point behind it.

Chapter 1 gives us an important clue to the time in which the novel is set. Maycomb County (like the rest of America) had been told, by its President, Franklin D Roosevelt, in his inaugural speech on **4 March 1933**, that "the only thing we have to fear is fear itself".

This was a reference to a banking crisis, itself a product of the Great Depression. Roosevelt was a Democrat, with liberal instincts. He was still President when he died in 1945, and many Americans regard him as one of the greatest two or three Presidents in their history. His wife Eleanor became a pioneer of **the human rights movement** in America- she is **referred to, insultingly, by the ladies of Maycomb, in Chapter 24.**

The opening is rather unconventional, and daring, in its lack of a strong sense of action- but is the point that **Maycomb itself is passive, slow, downtrodden and uncomfortably hot**- not just because of its weather, but because of its **sinfulness** (in its tendency to shoot mockingbirds)? First, we have a reported conversation between Scout, Jem (and Atticus), about who "started it all"- the events which led to Jem breaking his arm. This veers off into a detailed account of the Finch family, its history and the locality it lives in. Then we have the arrival of Dill, but the account of the children's activities, including Dill's dare to Jem to touch the Radleys' house, is interrupted by a long and detailed history of the Radleys and the **myths** about Boo.

The narrative reflects on the state of the economy- "there was nothing to buy and no money to buy it with".

Jem is aged thirteen when the novel ends, but almost ten in this first chapter- so he was born in 1923. Scout is nearly six (born 1927) and Dill is nearly seven (born 1926). Harper Lee was born in

April 1926, and Dill is modelled on her friend, the writer Truman Capote (born 1924). Maycomb is a fictional version of Lee's home town, Monroeville, in Alabama. Atticus is "nearly fifty" in Chapter 10, so he would have been born in or around 1884, and his wife in 1899. They were married in 1922, and she died of a heart attack in 1929.

Much of this opening chapter deals with the Finch family background, and with the mystery of the Radleys, who will form the sub-plot of the novel.

The **Finches are immigrants (like the African Americans)- they are Anglo- Americans**. Simon Finch was a Methodist who came to Alabama, indirectly, from Cornwall. He lapsed in regard to some of the rules of Methodism, bought three slaves, built a house, married, had daughters, and died, wealthy, at a great age.

The Finch family tradition was broken by Atticus, who took a law degree (his brother, Uncle Jack, went to Boston to train as a doctor and Atticus paid for his training, for a number of years); he left his sister, Alexandra, to live in the ancestral home, which is twenty miles from Maycomb. Atticus' tendency to go against the grain of tradition was an early characteristic!

Chapter 2

The narrative moves on to **September**; Dill has left, and Scout starts school. We find a relaxed and amused but **critical account of primary school teaching**, discipline, and its unworldly approach to dealing with children who have no money for lunch and no educational aspirations.

There is humour in the clash of cultures; teachers are suspicious about children reading and writing out of school, because they believe it has to be taught, slowly, chaotically, over several years, and without ambition. Scout's teacher, Miss Fisher, is naïve; she has no idea about the rural poverty of the Cunninghams. She condemns Atticus' approach as damaging, because he (and Calpurnia) cannot possibly have taught Scout to read and write properly, using the approved method. Her snobbery is accidental, but it is real all the same. Atticus' unconventional but effective way of reading with Scout is the same as his unconventional way of applying the law and accelerating change.

Scout gives her an eloquent explanation of the Cunninghams' way of life- not borrowing what they cannot pay back, and living within their means. This allows Harper Lee to expand on the theme of **rural poverty**. The plight of the farmers means that there is no cash in the community; Walter Cunningham Snr pays Atticus in stovewood, hickory nuts, smilax and holly and turnips instead.

He is eligible to take a state-funded job under the WPA (Works Progress Administration) scheme, which created work for unemployed people; 1.65 million destitute farmers were eligible. But he has chosen to keep farming, because a paid state-sponsored job would take him away from his land for 30-40 hours per week. All the people of Maycomb, except the villainous Ewells, have a certain pride in their heritage.

The end of this chapter leaves Scout's teacher unable to cope. There is a sarcastic treatment here of the progressive primary school teaching ethos championed by John Dewey. Scout has been taught to read and write long before she goes to school. Such pre-school adventures should be encouraged. Official teaching theory only ensures that the school is teaching the white children of Maycomb nothing. School is a major disappointment for both Scout and Jem.

Chapter 3

 Jem invites Walter home for lunch, and, as they talk on the way from school, Walter's defensiveness (because of his acute poverty) melts. The poor children eat syrup (molasses) with everything, and Walter pours it on to his meat and vegetables.

Calpurnia is "furious" with Scout for the disrespect she has shown Walter over his table manners; he is "just a Cunningham", and the Finches may be "better" than him. But, as a guest, he must be treated with respect, and allowed to eat in whatever way he likes.

Scout complains to Atticus that Cal prefers Jem to her. **Atticus trusts Cal completely and** relies on her as much as he does on anyone, including his sister. He **treats her** less as a servant than **as a fully entitled member of the Finch family.**

Back at school, Miss Fisher is terrified when a "cootie" crawls out of a boy's hair. That boy is Burris Ewell. When she tells him to go home, de-louse his hair and have a bath, he points out that he only comes to school for this one day each year. He is ready to pick a fight with Miss Fisher and with his class-mates; he calls her a "snot-nosed slut". Polite manners, and believing in personal hygiene and the value of education, seem of little use when people are living in such squalor as the Ewells.

Later, Atticus explains to Scout that such people have to be treated differently from everyone else, because they are outside the mainstream. The law against poaching means that Ewell should be prosecuted, but doing that would leave his children to starve. Ironically, no-one except Atticus and Link Deas has any thought for the effect on Tom Robinson's family of how the law is applied to him; and he is innocent!

That evening, we see, for the first time, **Atticus's way of handling problems**- in this case, the prohibition on reading at home for Scout. The first thing to do, to co-exist comfortably with all kinds of people, is to **see things as those others see them**; "climb into his skin and walk around in it".

Amusingly, Atticus lapses into legalese, and speaks to Scout as if she were an adult rather than a six-year-old child. But he understands both his children and their interests and anxieties, much better than they might think.

Chapter 4

The opening paragraph tells us more about the teaching methods in the primary school system- and how dull it is. Strictly, this has little to do with the plot, except to reinforce the point that Atticus needed no primary school as the foundation of his career. **There is no real education to be had in Maycomb; certainly, no education that racism and segregation are wrong**. We will see this in Chapter 26.

Someone (Boo Radley) leaves chewing gum, and then, on the last day of the summer term, two pennies, in a knot-hole in one of the oak trees on the boundary of the Radleys' garden.

Jem (like Walter, in the previous chapter) believes, superstitiously, that you will die if you touch anything in the Radleys' garden. That fear is not justified. On the other hand, Tom Robinson should fear that he will- literally- die, if he sets foot in the Ewells' garden- even though he does that by invitation and to be helpful.

We are now a year on from Chapter 1. Dill returns, heavier but no taller; the mystery of his father continues. Dill says he is president of the L&N railroad, and has a pointed black beard (he retracts the beard idea in the next chapter).

Jem rolls Scout in a tyre which ends up in the Radleys' garden. It is held back until the end of the chapter, but Scout has heard **low laughter in the Radleys'** house; **Boo is watching them, and wants to join in their games**. He would like to reach out to them, because he is essentially a child himself; but he is confined to the house because of his mental illness.

Jem invents the Boo Radley game; he thinks Boo must be dead by now. Scout disagrees, and is in the game reluctantly, and anxiously. The game turns into a play, with dialogue and a plot, as the summer proceeds. It is made from "gossip and neighbourhood legend". The children stop when adults appear; Miss Maudie Atkinson has some idea of its subject matter; Atticus catches them, and Jem denies the game is to do with the Radleys. **The trial, too, will be played out in public, and its plot will have no more of a basis in reality than the children's imaginings**. But Atticus will not be able to give instructions there, about how to treat Tom, in the way he can tell his children to treat other people with respect, and not misrepresent them.

The idea of letting children be children, while preparing them for the grown up world, is important to the novel. Aunt Alexandra's attempts to make Scout into a perfumed, starched, dry and gossipy little example of "Southern womanhood" have little value; she has already turned her grandson into the most boring child Scout has ever met, and a racist. Atticus wants his children to play, where there is no harm in it; he wants to protect them from danger (the lynch mob) but not from what is frightening or brave (Mrs Dubose, the trial). He wants them to treat Boo as an adult, and with respect, but **perhaps it is because of their efforts to "make him come out"- to reach out to him from one 'child' to another- that he is motivated to rescue them, when the time comes.**

Chapter 5

Miss Maudie Atkinson starts to talk to Scout in the evenings. She explains that "old Mr Radley was a foot-washing Baptist", who believed that anything of pleasure is a sin. This introduces **the problem of extreme or fundamentalist belief, and rigidity in opinions- "you can look down the street and see the results".** It may also explain the Radleys' taste for privacy; they have no desire to engage with the wider world.

Jem and Dill plan to deliver a note to Boo Radley on a fishing rod; they will push it through the shutters or make it stick on the window-sill at the side of the house. The pole is too short. Atticus tells them to stop tormenting Boo; he has a right to stay in his house, and they have no right to act out his "life's history" on the public street.

Jem admits the content of the Boo Radley game, accidentally; and he realises that Atticus has extracted the truth by using "the oldest lawyer's trick on record"- **provoking him into feeling he has to justify himself, and so revealing what he had no intention of saying. This prefigures Atticus's way of questioning Bob Ewell and Mayella Ewell in Chapters 17 and 18.**

Chapter 6

Dill is going home the following day (it is the end of his second summer in Maycomb). He and Jem plan to see whether they can catch a view of Boo Radley through the window with the loose shutter. Scout is goaded into going with them. Dill cannot see anything through the window. The boys try the back window; their steps make the wooden porch step squeak.

Scout sees a "shadow of a man with a hat on" which comes within a foot of Jem, raises and drops its arm, says nothing, and walks back round the side of the house. As the children retreat, there is the sound of **a shotgun blast**. Jem has to leave his trousers behind, to get under the fence to safety. There is **an element of terror** here which prepares for **the shooting of Tom Robinson as he tries to escape from prison- an event which Atticus reports in chapter 24**. Jem and Tom are similar in this threat of being shot, as well as being linked, eventually, by the restricted or non-use of their left arm.

When Scout and Jem get home, Mr Nathan Radley is at the front of his house with his gun; the neighbours, including Atticus, have all come out to see what the disturbance was. Dill invents the tall tale that Jem is not wearing his trousers because he won them from him in a game of strip poker; having sent the children away, Atticus soothes Dill's Aunt Rachel's outrage.

That creative lie still leaves Jem's trousers in the Radleys' garden, so, once the adults are asleep, he has to go to retrieve them, even under the stated threat that Mr Radley will shoot the next intruder he hears. **Jem prefers to run the risk of being shot** to the prospect of having to explain the lie to Atticus. When he returns, he says nothing, but Scout can hear his bed trembling from his sense of shock at his very narrow escape. It isn't until **Chapter 10** that **the idea of shooting and killing mockingbirds (harmless, unarmed and defenceless creatures) comes up; Jem was not so far away, here, from becoming the first mockingbird in the novel!**

Chapter 7

Scout now starts her second year at school; there is still no reading or writing. A week later, Jem tells her that when he went back for his trousers they had been picked up and folded, and left on the fence for him to collect. The tears had been sewn up, but not properly, but "crooked". Jem is worried that the Radleys may be able to read his mind, if they can anticipate what he will do. Now there is a ball of grey string in the hiding place in the tree.

In October, two soap carvings (one of Scout and one of Jem) are waiting for them in the tree. The detail is very realistic; they can only have been made by **someone who watches them closely**. The children will be **rescued** from Bob Ewell's attempt to murder them **only because Boo continues to watch them closely and protectively** throughout the novel- a point emphasised towards the end of the last chapter of the novel, where Scout stands on the Radleys' porch, and imagines the sights Boo has seen, all involving "his" children.

Within a fortnight, there is more chewing gum; then, another week later, a spelling medal, and, after that, a broken watch with a chain, and an aluminium knife.

They write a thank you note and intend to leave it in the tree- but the hole is filled up with cement. They look out for Mr Nathan Radley, who says that he has plugged the tree with cement because it is dying. Atticus thinks the tree is healthy. He is right; the tree is still growing, in Chapter 26.

We are left to deduce that **Boo Radley is trying to join in the children's games**, from a distance, and that **Nathan Radley** has found out, and stopped up the hiding place, because he **disapproves** of **Boo's attempts to have contact with the outside world, and to play games**. To feet-washing Baptists like Nathan Radley, the idea of fun is a sin.

Chapter 8

Mrs Radley dies that winter, but it is only mentioned in passing. Scout is alarmed, comically, at the sight of snow- the first snow in Maycomb County for almost 50 years (since 1885). She and Jem are allowed to take Miss Maudie Atkinson's snow to make a snowman. Jem sculpts it to look like Mr Avery, who has told them that the bad weather is caused by the bad behaviour of children. Atticus admires Jem's resourcefulness, but tells him he must modify its appearance, in order to avoid giving offence.

After one o'clock that night, a fire starts in Miss Maudie's house (which is made of wood, with a tin roof); the fire engine and its hose are both disabled by the extreme cold. The men all rescue as many of her possessions as they can. The fire engine from Abbottsville arrives in time to save the Finch house (and Miss Haverford's) by pouring water on the parts which smoke is reaching. Another fire truck comes from sixty miles away.

While Atticus joined in the rescue operation, Jem and Scout watched, standing outside the Radleys'. Mysteriously, someone has put a blanket over Scout to keep her warm. Jem thinks it must be Mr Nathan Radley, but Atticus identifies the person who noticed she was cold as Boo.

Chapter 9

This – **the longest chapter so far- introduces racism**, and presents it as **an attitude which is adopted, unthinkingly, even by white children of Scout's age- Cecil Jacobs and Francis Hancock.**

The other theme is Aunt Alexandra's disapproval of what she sees as Atticus' slack, rather than relaxed, way of bringing up his children. She finds them worryingly unconventional- although she says very little about this directly. She has plenty more to say about it once she comes to stay in Maycomb, just before the trial starts (Chapter 13 onwards).

The chapter has three scenes- Scout's confrontation with Cecil, their Christmas day at Finch Landing, and their Christmas evening at home, where **Atticus talks about the Tom Robinson case as already a lost cause, before it has even begun.**

Scout instinctively wants to fight, when her father is criticised in the playground as a defender of "niggers". Scout asks Atticus what the issue is; he tells her not to use that "common" word. Does he defend them? "Of course I do". He explains that **there is some "high talk" that Tom Robinson is not entitled to a defence, Atticus is taking the case because, if he did not, he could not represent the county in the state legislature, would feel his** reputation was lost, and would not be able to tell his own children what to do, because his moral integrity and authority would be gone.

He wants Scout to ignore the "ugly talk" and keep out of fights. **Although he will try to win the case, he knows that it is hopeless**. But the case is, somehow, a fight between "friends", and, however bitter it becomes, "they're still our friends and this is still our home".

She manages to resist more taunts at school, only to lose patience three weeks later, when Francis makes the same provocative insults. This is on the occasion of the traditional Christmas Day visit to Finch Landing, to eat Aunt Alexandra's cooking.

Scout has started experimenting, for a week, with swear words ("damn" and "hell"), to provoke an adult reaction, and in the hope that if her father believes she has learned them at school, he will agree to keep her at home. Alabama has a "ladies' law" which makes swearing within female earshot a criminal offence; it does not cater for girls and women who swear, themselves!

Atticus had ordered air-guns for both children, for Christmas, at their request, but he says they must use them responsibly, that they cannot take them to Alexandra's, and that Uncle Jack will have to teach them how to shoot with them. He **seems unenthusiastic about them having guns**, but sees their interest in them as "inevitable".

In the next chapter, we learn that **he told Jem that he would prefer him to shoot only at tin cans, but that if he will (inevitably) shoot at birds he must remember that "it's a sin to kill a mockingbird"**.

Miss Maudie explains that mockingbirds have a pleasing song, and cause no trouble. Because they're never aggressive, they should not be persecuted.

Francis says that "Uncle Atticus is a nigger-lover", and that, according to Alexandra, this damages their family's reputation, quite apart from his habit of letting his children "run wild". These comments do sound uncannily like her! When he repeats the term three times, Scout (understandably) punches him in the mouth. **Her aunt and Uncle Jack are prejudiced against Scout because of her swearing (this anticipates the fact that Tom Robinson cannot have a fair hearing, because the jury cannot see beyond his colour)**; **she is** taken home in disgrace, having been **found guilty of causing the fight, without the adult "jury" considering the evidence properly.**

Scout shows Jack, later, that he and Atticus were wrong to judge that she "had that coming to her"- in fact **(like Tom Robinson) she has resisted provocation as far as anyone could be expected to.**

Just as Jem had risked being shot in the Radley's back garden, so that Atticus would not think less of him for lying about his trousers, so Scout asks Jack not to tell him the real reason for the fight with Francis; she does not want him to think that she was unable to walk away from the kind of provocation he had asked her to resist.

Finch Landing is an eccentric house, which Simon Finch built so that his daughters could not come or go without his knowledge (he had eight daughters, and one son, called Welcome). At home, when Scout overhears her father and Uncle Jack discussing her, and the Robinson case, Atticus knows she is listening.

He says that she is growing up well, despite her tendency to be hot-headed, but that **both children "will have to absorb some** ugly things pretty soon". He explains to Jack that a jury will always take the Ewells' word against "a black man's", but that he hopes he may win the case on appeal. This means that he sees the prejudice and ignorance of the ordinary jurors of Maycomb as an obstacle which the legal process may be able to overcome- but not in Maycomb itself. Atticus says that racism is "Maycomb's usual disease", and that it is "mad", or rabid- in other words, the perfect place for a mad or rabid dog to walk through, in the next chapter!

Chapter 10

This chapter addresses **the children's prejudice that Atticus,** because he is an older parent, **is "feeble".** Miss Maudie points out that age fifty is not very old; that if they had a younger father they would not have the benefit of Atticus's age- his wisdom; and that there's life in him yet.

The talents which Maudie says Atticus has- being able to play a Jew's harp, and being the best draughts player in Maycomb- do not impress Scout. Calpurnia believes he can do all sorts of things, but cannot itemise them. The fact is that Atticus is the only father who will not play in a touch-football match between the Baptists and the Methodists.

The main part of this chapter shows what **Atticus is good at**- his **marksmanship** with a rifle, when the rabid dog, Tim Johnson, is on the street, one Saturday in February. Cal is panic-stricken and calls Atticus, to bring him home from his office; then she alerts everyone else of the danger, including the Radleys (who do not acknowledge her knocking and shouting).

Atticus arrives with Heck Tate. They agree that the dog has an infectious disease. Mad dogs are expected to behave more aggressively, and to be mad in August. This is a quiet, February madness, and the dog is pathetic. Atticus tells Heck Tate to shoot the dog, and he sends Cal and the children indoors. But Heck Tate asks Atticus (whom he calls "Mr Finch") to fire the shot, because it needs to be "a one-shot job" and, if he misses, the bullet might hit the Radleys'.

Atticus protests that it is thirty years since he fired a gun. He accidentally drops his glasses, which break, but **he shoots the dog with astonishing ease and accuracy**. Jem is shocked into an admiring, uncomprehending silence, because it takes him ten minutes to line up a target with his air gun. Atticus and Heck go to get Zeebo to collect the dead dog and disinfect the area. Miss Maudie calls him "One-shot Finch", and tells the children that he used to be the deadest shot in Maycomb County, and that, as a boy, he regarded missing once in fifteen shots as a failure.

She goes on to explain why Atticus has not mentioned his talent for shooting, or kept it up- **he is "civilized in his heart", and does not want to make use of a talent which amounts to "an unfair advantage over most living things".**

Fairness- to everyone- is what elevates Atticus above the other inhabitants of Maycomb, and the importance of fairness is central to the way he brings up his own children. It is also part of the reason why he could not leave Tom to be defended weakly in court, by the town's junior barrister Maxwell Green (see Chapter 22), regardless of the fact that his case is prejudiced from the start. This is a point taken from the criticism of the inadequately prepared defence in the first of the Scottsboro trials.

Miss Maudie says that "people in their right minds never take pride in their talents". The point is not lost on Jem. Now he understands that being superior is different from appearing superior to other people. If you have read Dickens' novel "Great Expectations", you will already be familiar with this idea.

Atticus' shooting of the mad dog has a symbolic meaning. He takes aim and fires at the "usual madness" of Maycomb- the equally crazy and crazed fever of racism- in the courtroom, but he cannot shoot it dead.

At the end of Chapter 21, when the case is lost, Scout has this exact image of her father in her mind- of him trying to fire a gun without ammunition. Atticus has the skill to shoot racism dead, but not the bullet he needs. That bullet is the change which only the younger generation can bring about.

Chapter 11

After Scout's trouble in resisting provocation, the children now have to run the gauntlet of Mrs Dubose's acid comments when they run past her house to meet their father each evening. Atticus tells Jem that she is both old and ill, and that he must not **"let her make you mad"**.

The day after Jem's twelfth birthday (a Saturday), towards the end of the summer term, he and Scout are going to the shops, when she is particularly unpleasant to them, and goes on to denounce Atticus for "lawing for niggers". She says that this is a betrayal of his family, and that he is "no better than the niggers and the trash he works for".

As with Scout's fights with Cecil and Francis, it is **an insult to Atticus** (and also blaming the death of their mother for their being bad) which **provokes Jem**. On the way back from the shops, he takes the baton he bought for Scout, uses it to vandalise Mrs Dubose's flowers, and then snaps it. It is a violent outburst, provoked by the demand to maintain a degree of self-control and perspective beyond a pre-teen child.

Jem has to answer to Atticus for his behaviour, in the way he had been so desperate to avoid, at the time of pestering the Radleys. Atticus says it is one thing for Jem to be annoyed by children saying that he "lawed for niggers and trash", but that there is no justification for vandalising the garden of a sick old lady.

Atticus is teaching both of his children the value of self-control under extreme provocation; that we should be scrupulously fair to others, and make allowances for their bad behaviour, even when they are ludicrously unfair to us.

How different is the persecution and hounding Scout and Jem each experience from the vicious racial cruelty Tom has to endure?

The answer is, not at all! It is just the same. And who else maintains their self-control, is fair to others, and makes allowances for their bad behaviour? Tom Robinson, when he is trapped by Mayella Ewell.

Atticus tells Scout that remaining level-headed will be more demanding later that summer, and that, while "it's not fair" for children to have to be under this degree of pressure, **what is important is "the way we conduct ourselves when the chips**

are down"- when we incur the scorn and insults of the whole community we live in.

The difference between Scout's point of view and Atticus' lightens the tone a little. She thinks that when he sends Jem to speak to Mrs Dubose he will be murdered; Atticus has already talked the situation through with Mrs Dubose, and he knows how close to dying she is.

For Atticus, defending Tom Robinson is "the essence of a man's conscience", and a matter of personal ethical standards. He "couldn't go to church and worship God" if he did not accept the task of representing Tom.

When Jem comes back, Atticus says that Mrs Dubose cannot be held responsible for what she says and does, because she is ill and old- it seems that, like the Ewells being exempted from rules about truancy and poaching, allowances have to be made here too.

Jem has to make amends by reading to Mrs Dubose for two hours each day for a month. The reader shares Jem's sense that this is a tyrannical demand- we only find out later that it is part of Mrs Dubose's brave battle to prepare for her own death.

The rest of this chapter- which brings to a close the first part of the novel- describes the horror of the reading sessions. It is rather like the tale of Little Red Riding Hood, with Mrs Dubose as the wolf masquerading as the grandmother.

Finally, **Scout asks Atticus what the term "nigger-lover" means-** the insult she has fought over, because of the way it was said (by Francis, and by Mrs Dubose).

Atticus says that it is used by "ignorant, trashy people" who feel that Negroes are being favoured over them. The insult, therefore, reflects badly on the person who says it.

After a month, Atticus comes to see her while the children are still at the reading session with Mrs Dubose. The old lady demands a further week; the sessions are long now, because she does not need her medicine so often. More than a month later, she dies. Atticus explains to the children that he knew she was dying, because he had drawn up her Will; and that the reading was part of the process by which she wanted to break her dependence on pain-killers, a courageous and painful ambition. She left Jem a flower as a sign of forgiveness and reconciliation.

Atticus would have sent the children to read to her in any event, because **he wanted them to witness "real courage", not backed up with the force of a gun, but facing death, or defeat, bravely- even though you know it is both unfair and inevitable.**

This is a telling point to end Part One with, because Atticus knows that, in defending Tom Robinson, he is beaten before he starts. Knowing that you will lose your case, or that your efforts will not affect the outcome, is no excuse for not being brave.

Atticus' innate talent as a marksman- his ability to shoot a dog cleanly- does not signify courage. Real courage lies in the peaceful resistance of aggression (such as refusing to retaliate when Bob Ewell spits at him at the start of Chapter 23, and facing down the gang in Chapter 15) when you are weak or feeble. Atticus' calm and dignified refusal to condone what is wrong is very similar to the non-violent protests, such as the Alabama bus boycott of 1956, which altered the course of history, as well as featuring prominently as a theme in this novel. It also prefigures the account of the events which have put Tom on trial; he offered only peaceful resistance to Mayella Ewell's sexual approach to him. He is accused of a violent assault but he is not violent in the least.

Part Two

Chapter 12

The summer starts with Jem becoming an adolescent and Dill writing to announce he will not be visiting, because he has "a new father". Atticus is called away for two weeks for an emergency session of the state legislature- there are sit-down strikes in Birmingham, and bread lines in the cities grow longer. Because he is away, Calpurnia suggests that she takes Jem and Scout to her church.

She makes extraordinarily detailed preparations so that no one can criticise the way she presents them. What follows is a long and vivid description of First Purchase African M.E. Church. Jem and Scout are welcomed and treated with respect, except by Lula, who believes in segregation, and about whom the same word is used- "contentious"- as was used of the Ewells, especially Bob Ewell, in Chapter 3.

For a minute or two, Jem and Scout feel what it is like to be excluded from society, unwelcome, outsiders.

This is the condition of society in Maycomb. Calpurnia refutes Lula's assertion that the churches should be segregated by race, like everything else (including the graveyards) by saying that there is only one God. **Calpurnia is like Atticus; she stands for an inclusive society which treats everyone fairly.**

The church is a place where the black community supports its vulnerable citizens- the collection for the next four weeks is to support the Robinson family, and, despite the poverty of its members, it raises a significant sum (ten dollars); almost through forcing people to make sacrifices, the most needy are provided for from within their own community. The prayers, too, are directed at specific cases of need, not generalised platitudes; and the sermon uses the current behaviour of real people to illustrate its points, and galvanise the community in a positive way.

This practical application of religion- for social good in its own community- is in marked contrast with the sterile, self-congratulating religion of the ladies in the missionary society in Chapter 24. The warmth, dignity and **vivid colourfulness of First Purchase** is very different from **the pale "fragile pastel" colours the white women wear**. They are preoccupied with the pecking order of devoutness (Mrs Merriweather first, Mrs Farrow second).

Zeebo, the rubbish collector, who disposed of the dead dog, is the music superintendent, who leads the singing of hymns by a congregation which cannot read. Calpurnia says that she is one of only four of the congregation who can read; she learnt reading from Miss Maudie's aunt. In the Ewell family, only Mayella and her father can read. Illiteracy is a sign of trashiness among white people; in the black community, it is the consequence of a lack of opportunity.

The lines of hymn 273 form part of the narrative. It ends on a melancholy or sad and reflective note. The words are to do with **the vision of a better life (after death) on a faraway shore; metaphorically, this is a dream of a world without the burden**

of prejudice and oppression. There is a wide river to be crossed before these people can live a contented life; and they have no means of crossing it in the near future.

The reason for the collection- so that Tom Robinson's wife Helen can provide for her children- prompts Scout to ask why she cannot take them to work in the fields. This brings the disclosure (from Calpurnia) that Tom has been accused of rape, so that it is taboo to employ Helen. The Rev Sykes has described Atticus as the church's best friend (which is why his children are so welcome) and Scout remembers Atticus' description of the Ewells (Tom's accusers) as "absolute trash".

Calpurnia deflects the children's request for a definition of the term rape to their father, and they go on to ask her why she speaks differently among coloured people from how she speaks in Maycomb. They regard their own way of speaking as better.

She **points out that it is necessary to speak the language of the people you are with, unless you want to alienate them.** Scout now starts to develop a genuine interest in seeing Calpurnia's native culture, by visiting her at her home. Calpurnia says she is welcome, any time. Aunt Alexandra is obstructive about this, but, when Atticus takes Calpurnia to tell Helen that Tom has been shot, Jem and Dill are in the car. Only the Finch family will set foot in "the Quarters", the settlement down the track past the Ewells' shack and the dump where the black people in the novel live.

Calpurnia's chameleon-like flexibility with language is really the same as Atticus' dogma that, to get on with other people, you have to climb into their skin and see things from their point of view (Chapter 3). If the jury could see things as Tom had seen them, there would be no miscarriage of justice.

They return from church to Maycomb to the unwelcome sight of Aunt Alexandra sitting "upright, uncompromising" in a rocking chair on their porch- an unwelcome and unexpected arrival from their own culture.

The Rev Sykes has the power to extract the required amount from the church collection by having the doors locked, and he can challenge and force individuals (Carlow Richardson) and groups (people without children) to make up the shortfall. The **Rev Sykes and the Finch children meet again, at the courthouse, which is, in a sense, Atticus' church (Chapters 16-21).**

Atticus should have the same power and moral force there- but the prejudice of white Maycomb denies him the power to make his congregation (the jury) do the right thing. The white community is lacking in morality, care and a proper sense of responsibility.

Scout assumes, naively, that because Tom is in prison he *must have* done something very bad. Calpurnia points out that what people say and what he is accused of are making it impossible for Helen to find work. **Scout's assumption that accusation and guilt are the same thing is endemic in the white adult community**- even though, as Scout herself recognises, an accusation made by the Ewells is hardly worth giving any credence to.

Chapter 13

Alexandra announces that she and Atticus decided it was time that she came to stay with them. She speaks in instructions. She declares that Scout will become "interested in clothes" and therefore needs "some feminine influence". Scout remembers that her aunt once told Atticus that she was "sluggish".

Atticus drives back from his work visit to Montgomery; he confirms that Alexandra's arrival is something they both agreed on, because Atticus will be busy (with the trial) and **"the summer's going to be a hot one"- he is really referring to the (racist) atmosphere, rather than the weather**.

Alexandra is an unlovable, snobbish and uncompromising or dictatorial figure who **takes the warmth and informality out of the children's home.** She sends Atticus to tell them that they should develop a sense of pride in their family history (even though their cousin Joshua S St Clair had tried to assassinate the President!). Her message- via him- is that they are a family of good breeding, so that they must behave "like the little lady and gentleman that you are".

All three –Scout, Jem and Atticus- are **uncomfortable with Alexandra's snobbery and formality.** Atticus tells them to forget it, but he does not want them to rebel against it. It is another compromise, of the sort he made with Scout over reading- sometimes we can and should do what we think is best, and simply avoid offending others, while we disregard their demands on us.

Scout cannot understand Alexandra's preoccupation with their family roots, which she uses to reassure herself of her own family's superiority, and to justify her own settled and fixed opinions.

Atticus and his brother, Uncle Jack, judge people on their merits, not their family history. Both men are inclined to believe that the whole of the human race originated in Africa, and that all attempts to differentiate our origins are pointless.

Chapter 14

Scout and Jem are hearing uncomplimentary mutterings about them when they go out. Scout asks Atticus what rape is. He gives the lawyer's definition- "carnal knowledge of a female by force and without consent". This is a signpost for the reader, as much as Scout, of the subject of the trial.

Atticus is relaxed about Calpurnia's trip to her church with the children, but **Alexandra disapproves and forbids the visit to Calpurnia's home**. Atticus shows a united front with his (racist) sister this time. But when she accuses him of being soft, and suggests that they should sack Calpurnia, that is one step too far. Atticus protests that **Calpurnia is "a faithful member of this family"** and that she will stay working for them for as long as she likes.

This is a graphic example of Atticus's colour-blindness confronting his own sister's prejudice.

The rest of the chapter is taken up with the surprise appearance of Dill, who is hiding under Scout's bed. He claims to have been imprisoned by his new father, and to have escaped via a travelling circus. He is worried he will be being searched for. Jem reveals Dill to Atticus, who does not intend to surrender him to his aunt Rachel but will ask her for permission for Dill to stay that night.

In truth, Dill has run away from home, because his mother and his stepfather showed no interest in him, and he feels in their way.

Chapter 15

Dill is allowed to stay. A week later, the tension over the trial begins to dominate the narrative.

On Saturday evening, Heck Tate knocks on the door, and Atticus has to go outside to speak to a group of men who are with him. Tom Robinson is being moved to the prison in the middle of Maycomb the next day, in anticipation of the start of the trial, and Mr Tate is worried there may be a violent protest of some kind. He is reluctant to house Tom Robinson.

Atticus doubts there will be any trouble. The trial should start on Monday, and on Sundays there is church-going, not drinking. Mr Link Deas says that any violence will come not from Maycomb people but from "that Old Sarum bunch" (the out of town Cunninghams)- this is significant, because the jury will be drawn from this group, the most rabidly racist part of white society.

Atticus is completely unafraid because he thinks that decency will prevail (he is wrong, for once). When Mr Deas tells him that he should not have accepted the case, because he has "everything to lose", Atticus puts his killer question to him- "Do you really think so?".

It is a question he always asks when someone is wrong about something. **He says to Mr Deas "you know what the truth is" (that Tom Robinson is innocent).**

We do not understand the significance of this remark until later- Mr Deas has employed Tom and always found him completely decent and reliable.

Jem senses an aggressive confrontation, but Atticus tells him that the people had come to warn him of the potential for some type of confrontation. **He tells Jem that there has never been a gang in**

Maycomb; we know this is not strictly true, because Boo Radley was caught up with a gang of sorts when he was a boy. Jem is worried that Atticus may be the target for aggression.

Jem says that there was a Ku Klux Klan which persecuted Catholics once; Atticus says that there was such a group, in about 1920, but that it was political; disbanded; and would never return.

Scout overhears the end of another discussion in which Atticus is having to tell his sister that he would not leave Tom Robinson to be condemned to death, undefended, in order to maintain the **"polite fiction" that a black man accused of rape must be guilty**. Jem says that Alexandra has been arguing, again, that to defend him in court is a disgrace to the Finch family's reputation.

The next day- Sunday- sees more discussion involving Atticus, Heck Tate and a group of men. Tom Robinson has been brought to the town prison. In the evening, Atticus announces that he is going out; he takes an extension cable and a light bulb with him. Unusually, he goes out in the car.

Scout and Jem collect Dill and they follow at 10 pm to see what is going on. Atticus has parked the car outside his office, but he is sitting at the front door of the prison, with his light bulb rigged up to the car battery so that he can read the paper; he is there **to protect Tom Robinson, his client, from any gang**.

"Four dusty cars" arrive; Atticus has been expecting them. The gang is led by **Walter Cunningham**, who says they **want to take Tom from the cells (to kill him).** They claim that they have diverted Heck Tate into the countryside, so that there is no police protection; when they become threatening, Atticus asks them his question "do you really think so?". He means ,"do you really think that I will stand aside and let you take the law into your own hands, in the form of mob violence?".

Scout bursts on to the scene with Dill and Jem. The gang is not men Scout has seen before, but a group of country farmers, identified by "a smell of stale whisky and pig-pen". Atticus is afraid, but Jem will not obey his instruction to go home. The gang wants the children out of the way. Scout recognises Walter Cunningham Senior, and makes a persistent effort to strike up a friendly conversation with him about his legal affairs and his son. Mr Cunningham is disarmed by Scout's interest in him; his aggression subsides, and he stands the gang down.

Tom Robinson asks Atticus for reassurance that they have gone, in "a soft husky voice". Meanwhile, Mr Underwood has been protecting Atticus secretly, with his shotgun, in his upstairs office window (a reassuring detail, told only after the event, so that, during the event, we have the full dramatic impact of believing Atticus is unprotected and could be harmed).

Jem's refusal to be sent out of harm's way has enabled Scout to protect Atticus from a real threat. Atticus's earlier ideas and predictions- that his children cannot be kept immune from the ugly business of the trial, but that he hopes they can come through it undamaged- are beginning to be given substance, and justified, in the action of the novel.

Chapter 16

After this dramatic confrontation, **Scout** (aged nearly nine now) **associates her father's bravery in resisting the lynch mob with his bravery in shooting the dog;** the sense of danger is beginning to be oppressive.

Alexandra argues with Atticus that he should not mention other people's racist attitudes in front of Calpurnia, because it will be reported back to the black community, where it will

encourage resentment of the members of the white community he criticises.

Atticus maintains that she knows the truth of what he says already. He refuses to give in to his sister's artificial and prissy ways of behaving.

Scout and Jem ask Atticus how he can regard Walter Cunningham as a friend when he had wanted to harm him. Atticus excuses his aggression as the product of **"blind spots" and the mob instinct**; he praises the children for **defusing the tension by making Cunningham "stand in my shoes for a minute".** Scout threatens to exact revenge on Walter Jnr when they go back to school. Atticus tells her he does not want them to bear grudges, whatever happens with the trial. Alexandra says, gloomily, that she has warned him of the problems which allowing the children to be involved will cause.

From early in the morning, the outlying community drives in, on horses and in carriages, to reach the courthouse, to witness the trial. The morning is taken up with selecting the jury. Instead of showing us that not very dramatic scene, Harper Lee has Jem comment to Dill on **the various people who pass the house on their way to the town. They are all either obsessive and unbalanced, or eccentric**.

The children walk to the courthouse. The middle of the town is a picnic site, but it is **segregated by colour.**

There is an important discussion of skin colour among the children. To them, it is absurd that there should be any segregation; Uncle Jack says that, while the Finches have always been white, they may well have come from Africa in the ancient past.

To Scout, Jem and Dill, racism has no basis. They are dimly aware of Aunt Alexandra's assumption that the coloured community is full of gossip and sedition, but she is only a recent presence at home, and Atticus is naturally fair and even-handed in his approach to everyone. In Chapter 12, the brief but fractious appearance of Lula showed that **racism, or hostility towards outsiders, is not restricted to the white community; but Mrs Dubose (even though she employed a coloured maid), the (religious) Jacobs family, Mr Underwood, and Francis Hancock are all typical- most white children in Maycomb acquire racist attitudes from their parents and other adults.**

The deeply ingrained resistance to new thinking among the people of Maycomb is embedded in its buildings, too. The old courthouse burnt down in 1856, and its rebuilding around the concrete pillars which survived shows that this community is "determined to preserve every physical scrap of the past".

The very rare cases of behaviour which deviates from the norm- such as Dolphus Raymond's- has to be excused through **the cover of an extraordinary, gruesome and fantastic story** (his bride-to-be's suicide, pulling the trigger of a shotgun with her toes) – **just as the mythology of the Radleys fills the gap represented by the unknown or the misunderstood.**

Immediately after this demolition of the basis for racism, the trial starts. The black community, and Mr Raymond, have to wait and let the white families go in first; there are few women and children, because, for them, this is not a festive occasion, or a spectacle; it is a serious matter of life and death.

The Idlers' club- a group of elderly white men who watch all the trials as free entertainment- gossip about Atticus. They are typically racist too, but, from overhearing them, Scout finds out that Atticus has been appointed to defend Tom- he had no choice-but, having been given the (hopeless) task, he aims to do it to the best of his ability. While this is news to Scout, we have already known it.

Rev Sykes helps the three children to find seats, which are given up for them, on the front row of the coloured balcony, upstairs. **The jury appears to be made up of farmers (the most racist of all of the occupational groups in Maycomb, as the lynch mob showed),** and one or two of them may be Cunninghams- an indication that a fair trial is out of the question.

Chapter 17

The trial begins. Because we do not yet know any of the details, we are drawn into the drama as we read. All we know at this stage is that Tom is accused of rape; that the jury is racist; that Atticus expects to lose the case, but thinks an appeal against the sentence may succeed; and that the racist white community (including his own sister) disapproves of Atticus' defence of Tom.

Heck Tate is the first witness. He had been about to go home on the evening of November 21st when Bob Ewell arrived at his office, "very excited", claiming that "some nigger'd raped his girl" half an hour earlier. He found her on the floor of the room on the right, "pretty well beat up", and she said that it was Tom who had "hurt her" and "taken advantage of her". She identified him and Tate arrested him.

Atticus asks whether anyone called a doctor- Tate says that it wasn't necessary. This means that she was not badly hurt, and that **the accusation of rape was not verified at the time**. Atticus asks him three times, "just to make sure"- so that the slowest of juries cannot miss the point.

The injuries were bruises on her arms, and a developing black eye. Tate is careless about which eye- he says, first, that it was her left eye, then that it was her right eye. When Atticus pushes him on this, he blinks, "as if something had suddenly been made plain to him". This is that **Tom could not have inflicted those injuries, because he does not have the use of his left hand- a fact which we are not yet aware of.**

Tate says that there were finger marks *all around* her throat – another indication that these injuries were inflicted by someone left-handed, but with the full use of both his hands.

Jem has a grasp of the legal argument, which Scout does not- she sees only the lack of loud confrontation, while he **understands that there is no proof that the Ewell daughter was raped**.

Now we read a detailed description of the squalor the Ewells live in; and the sordid dirt and mess is in sharp contrast to the brief description of the "small Negro settlement some five hundred yards beyond the Ewells' "- a place kept neat and warm, with cooking smells; a civilised and peaceful community, unlike the Ewells' hovel, where the only housekeeping is Mayella's micro-garden of geraniums.

Asked if he is Mayella's father, Bob Ewell tries to make a tasteless joke; Judge Taylor warns him not to be "audibly obscene". He testifies that he was returning from the woods, just before dusk, when he heard Mayella, inside the house, screaming. He uses **animalistic language- her yells sounded "like a stuck hog", and he says he saw Tom, "that black nigger yonder ruttin' on my Mayella"**. Rev Sykes is concerned that the subject is unsuitable for children, but Jem refuses to leave, or to take Scout home.

Ewell is perversely self-satisfied with the distress he has caused the public gallery with this nakedly racist image. He confirms to Judge Taylor that he saw an actual rape take place. He says he saw through the window, then ran to the front of the house, where Tom ran out past him and escaped. He claims that the settlement down the track should be destroyed, because it devalues his house(!!) and it makes life "dangerous".

Atticus asks him why he did not call a doctor. **Ewell** says that there was no need to, because he had seen the perpetrator, and he never calls a doctor, because a visit costs five dollars. The second point is true, but the first **betrays his lack of concern for Mayella; or, rather, the truth, that there was no rape.**

After inviting Ewell to endorse Tate's evidence about which side of Mayella's face was bruised, **Atticus invites Ewell to write his name- which proves that he is left-handed. Only 11% of people are left-handed.** Again, Jem judges the evidence in a purely objective way, and concludes that Mayella was attacked by her own father.

Bob Ewell's excitement, when he ran to the sheriff, and his remark about having tried to have the settlement demolished for the past fifteen years, both explain his motivation.

A man like this would readily beat his daughter up in order to pervert the justice system and bring a false, opportunistic charge against the object of his racism. But those clues are so small, so apparently insignificant, that we barely notice them, on a first reading- like Scout and the audience at the trial, we focus only on the legal questions and answers.

At the end of the chapter, we are in the same position as Scout. We feel that the case does not change just because Bob Ewell is left-handed; Tom Robinson could also be left-handed. Moreover, any two-handed person could have used both hands in a physical attack.

Chapter 18

This should be the key moment for the prosecution, because the chapter is devoted to Mayella's evidence, and Atticus' careful dismantling of it. She is suspicious of Atticus because what she has to say is not the truth; she cries, before she speaks, in an attempt to persuade Judge Taylor to protect her from him. **The judge invites her to "tell the- tell us what happened to you"- notice the absence here of the word** *truth*. **He knows that expecting to hear that from her is to expect far too much.**

Her version of events is that she was on the porch when Tom came past. She asked him to break up a piece of furniture for firewood, and, when she went to get a coin to pay him with, he attacked her from behind, held her around her neck, hit her repeatedly, knocked her on to the floor, choked her and raped her. She claims to have fainted at the end of this.

Her account is "stealthy" and "steady-eyed", cat-like in its cunning. But Atticus undermines it. First, he asks questions which establish what life at the Ewells' is like, with too little to eat, no shoes, no routine. Nothing constructive to do. This is all done through indirect speech- we know it already, from the description of the household in the previous chapter.

Mayella has no friends- a key factor in her real motive for inviting Tom in, as we will discover in the next chapter. She lets slip the inference that her father drinks away most of his benefits, and that he can be violent when he is drinking. She denies that he has ever hit her.

It is only after he has cast doubt on the quality of her relationship with her father that Atticus questions Mayella about her evidence. She says that this was the first time she had invited Tom in, but then admits that she may have asked him to do other odd jobs before then. Atticus does not dwell on that; he returns to it in Tom's own evidence.

He presses her on the allegation that Tom punched her in the face; she says that he did, but that she cannot remember the details. **When Atticus asks her to identify Tom positively, and Tom stands up, everyone can see that he has a disability- his left arm is "dead", as a result of an accident in a machine when he was a child.** Atticus questions her further, once it is clear what Tom could or could not do; she has said that he choked her, and punched her, using his right fist to give her a black eye- her left eye- something it would be difficult to do. He asks her why she did not run away, and why, if she was screaming, her many brothers and sisters did not come to help her.

He suggests that she only screamed when she saw her father at the window, because there had been nothing to scream about; that *she screamed at her father, not at Tom*; and that it was her father who beat her. Atticus says that Tom was innocent, that he had "the best defence" to a charge of rape, because any aggression there was came from her to him, and that the violence was her father's, because he is a racist who would not tolerate her having any relationship with Tom.

Atticus' analysis of what really happened shocks and surprises us, because it is based on the defence he has prepared, with Tom- a defence of the truth, which Atticus already knows, but which we, as readers, have had no advance warning of.

Mayella's careful and deliberate lies have been exposed. Her response is "terror....fury....hatred". She refuses to answer any more questions.

Because the prosecution's case has now been put, there is a ten minute break. The time is approaching four o'clock; as Atticus has only one witness, presenting the defence case can be completed on this same day.

Chapter 19

Tom's defence is the plain and simple truth. Although Mayella's evidence (and her father's) has crumbled, under Atticus' questions, the facts he reveals- prompted by Atticus to tell the whole truth- are scandalous, in the sense that to accept the truth as truth would mean sweeping away the racial prejudice which makes Maycomb what it is.

<u>Tom tried to help Mayella, because he felt sorry for her; and the attempted sexual assault was on him, by her.</u>

We should feel prepared for these revelations, because **Harper Lee has already contrasted the living conditions of the black community and the Ewells, in order to show that the trash** here is white, hypocritical, and worthless- both outside society and unfit to be included in it.

It may be true that Bob Ewell has not assaulted Mayella physically until now- but there is one line in the text that suggests he has previously sexually assaulted her. When Tom Robinson describes what Mayella said to him, when she tells him that she has never kissed a grown man before, she adds the chilling – "what her papa do to her don't count".

So, from that, we can make the presumption that **when he finds his daughter taking an interest in someone else, Ewell is consumed with jealous anger (because, sickeningly, it is only him that she should kiss); and when he sees who it is, he is consumed with racist anger.**

Shockingly, we realise that it was not Tom he threatened to kill, but Mayella, whom he defined, on that occasion, as a whore!

The opening lines show that Tom cannot place his left hand on the Bible to take the oath in the normal way; it has already been brought to our attention, at the very start of the novel, that the arm Jem breaks, later, is his left arm, too.

The decent, respectable, and open-minded, of all colours, are united in their sympathies, and the disfigurements or injuries they bear- Jem, like Tom, will suffer at the hands of Bob Ewell's vicious hatred.

Tom is married; has three children; and once spent thirty days in prison after being in a fight and being unable to pay the court fine for it. He is a reliable employee of Mr Link Deas, who finds work for him throughout the year. He has to pass the Ewells' shack to go to and from his work, and so he often speaks to Mayella, but the furniture - chopping was more than a year ago, and he refused to take any money.

Mayella would continually find small jobs for him to do (because she was so lonely). He would never accept payment because he knew she had little money, and none to spare. He thought that the rest of her family gave her no help. As the narrator of this chapter, **Scout reflects that Mayella was as isolated and outcast as a creole child (of Spanish origin), and more than Boo Radley**. Tom was probably the only person who was ever polite to her (hence her liking him), but **she is lying, to condemn him (because of her father).**

Tom's evidence about the evening of 21st November is that, as he walked home, he noted how quiet it was. **Mayella had saved money for a year in order to send her seven siblings to buy ice cream- so that she could try to seduce Tom.**

This is an extraordinary amount of planning for anyone to do. But, in the same way that she has grown the geraniums in her pots - from seed and so slowly, with regular attention- she is capable of this. In another family (with a different father and upbringing), she would not need to make such a desperate plan, to overcome her incestuous isolation and loneliness.

Tom recalls telling her that saving for the ice cream was a clever thing to do- not because he welcomed the opportunity to be alone with her, but because she was being kind to her younger brothers and sisters.

She pretended that she needed Tom to mend a door; then, when she asked him to stand on a chair and bring down a box, she grabbed him, hugged him and kissed him. It was clear that **she intended a premeditated sexual experiment.** Despite the clumsiness of this bid to seduce him, Tom could not escape because he could not push past her; and that was the point when **Bob Ewell appeared- not, we should note, because she was being attacked, and screaming; not because she had been**

raped, but by accident. And it is because there was no possibility that she had been raped that he did not call a doctor. Instead, he beat her, half carrying out the threat he uttered as "you goddamn whore, I'll kill ya".

Mr Gilmer uses Tom's prison term for fighting as an indication of physical strength and a violent temperament; and he calls into question Tom's motive- that he felt sorry for Mayella, because she was trying to make some sort of effort at her life, unlike her family, and because she received no help from them.

The idea that the class system could be overturned like this- that a black man could be kind and helpful to a white woman- is unthinkable in Maycomb, because it strikes at the deepest roots of prejudice.

Tom's explanation- that he thought Mayella deserved to be helped- comes after Gilmer asks him twelve questions in a row, and calls him "boy" (a derogatory or insulting term) four times. Scout is right to note that Tom and Atticus share a rather quaint, but sincere, way of speaking to people.

Tom is more concerned not to shock the spectators in court than to protect himself in his defence. He does not accuse Mayella of lying, but says she is "mistaken in her mind".

The narrative tells us that Gilmer asks Tom a further ten questions, but Scout hears only the first seven (with two more uses of "boy"), before she has to leave the court room with Dill, who is crying, because Gilmer is being so "hateful" to Tom. Scout says that Tom is "just a Negro" – one of the few incidences of prejudice that we see in her - but Dill says it is sickening that *anyone* can be spoken to like this.

Chapter 20

There is more in this chapter about social attitudes and racism, from Mr Dolphus Raymond. His role in the novel is to widen the perspective on racism, and to show that a different approach is possible; but that **the only way you can be accepted, if you are open to mixed race relationships, is by excluding yourself from polite white society.**

He is known as "an evil man", a "sinful man", who appears to drink whisky continually, in a town which supports the prohibition of alcohol. But when he offers Dill a drink we are in for a surprise; it is neat Coca Cola, and the impression of a drunkard which he gives in public is an elaborate act.

He explains to Scout and Dill that, by cultivating this reputation, he can live as he likes, without attracting aggressive criticism. Because people see him as a pitiable alcoholic, they concede to him the freedom to live an unconventional life. The real alcoholic, incidentally, is Miss Rachel Haverford, Dill's aunt.

Mr Raymond believes that **the children will understand his reasons, because they are not yet used to the casual cruelty with which white people treat black people**, because they think of them as less than human.

The larger part of the chapter relates the closing part of **Atticus'** summing up to the jury. He is unusually and uncomfortably hot (because Tom faces a possible death sentence, if convicted). He **puts the argument as simply as he can. It is, he says, without intended irony, "as simple as black and white", in the sense that it hinges on the unreliable evidence of two white witnesses against the reliable testimony of a black defendant.**

He points out that there is no evidence that there was a crime of rape, and that Mayella has made the accusation because, having broken an unbreakable social rule- that white women should have nothing to do with black men- she would otherwise be cast out "as unfit to live with". However poor and ignorant she is, and however bad the assault on her by her father afterwards (a left-handed man), there is no excuse for making such obviously false allegations.

Atticus reminds the jury that Tom is quiet and respectable, and that his only offence was to feel sorry for Mayella and seek to help her; and that she and her father assume that Tom will be found guilty, automatically, simply on racial grounds, because the jury will be prejudiced against him, and will not believe him.

It is an "evil assumption" that all members of a race- any race- are bad and dangerous people; in fact, of course, bad people come from all racial groups.

He ends by reminding them that the jury system guarantees- or is supposed to guarantee- a fair trial, regardless of the defendant's background or position in society.

Chapter 21

Alexandra sends Atticus (via Calpurnia) a note saying that the children are missing. He discovers that they are in fact in the courthouse and so he sends them home, but allows them to come back later, to hear the verdict, if it has not been delivered already.

Jem, who judges the case simply on the merits of the evidence, is sure that Tom will be found not guilty. As Dolphus Raymond had observed, the children do not yet have enough experience to see how embedded racist is in the adult population.

Alexandra' sulky disapproval of Atticus' decision to allow the children back in court is apparent in what she does- she says nothing at all, and eats nothing.

Rev Sykes points out to Jem, who is buoyantly optimistic, that he has never "seen any jury decide in favour of a coloured man over a white man". The jury still has not decided the case by 11 pm- three and a half hours after it started discussing it.

Scout feels **cold**, despite the heat, **as if it is midwinter and "the mockingbirds were still".** Her mind is full of moments of tension and the surprise of experiencing dramatic events as a child- the fire which destroyed Miss Maudie's house, and Atticus shooting the dog, Tim Johnson. She feels empty. **This prepares us for the injustice of the verdict**. Atticus has done all he can, and he leaves through the public gallery; everyone in the coloured gallery stands up as he goes, as a sign of respect.

Chapter 22

Jem is outraged by the injustice of the verdict. Atticus is tired. Alexandra argues that the children should not have been exposed to the trial, but **Atticus says that they have been brought up to experience the world of Maycomb County as it is**, with its solid, unchanging racial prejudice alongside its avowed religiosity.

In the morning, the house is full of food, sent as a sign of their appreciation by Tom's father and people throughout the black community, despite their own poverty.

Miss Maudie has the three children round for cake, in an attempt to normalise life for them. She tells Jem not to worry about the outcome of the trial. Jem is disillusioned; he has seen, now, that Maycomb is not a warm "cocoon" populated by the best people in the world.

She points out that, in allocating the task of defending Tom to Atticus, Judge Taylor had done what he could to help Tom, because, by rights, he should have been given an inexperienced junior lawyer. She knew that even Atticus could not win the case, but, **by keeping the jury out**- by challenging their prejudices, and making it more difficult for them to return a 'guilty' verdict as a racist reflex- **he has made the community take a small step towards fairness.**

The unpleasant Miss Stephanie Crawford takes pleasure in telling the children that Bob Ewell has stopped Atticus in the street, spat in his face and threatened to kill him.

Chapter 23

This chapter is about the legal system and social attitudes. It is all conversation; the plot does not advance; there is no action. Atticus talks at greater length than elsewhere; see whether you find what he says in character, and convincing.

I feel that Harper Lee is rather intrusive here, reinforcing some of the messages we have already received in the chapters we have been reading.

Jem and Scout find Bob Ewell's threat to Atticus worrying. **From a child's perspective, they think of the practical consequences; if their father were dead, Alexandra would be in charge and would sack Calpurnia, and they would have no money. Some of these insecurities mirror the practical issues Tom Robinson's widow and children will face.**

Atticus refuses either to carry a gun or to arrange a restraining order. He judges that Ewell fees ashamed about being exposed at the trial as a daughter-beater, and that it is understandable that he should aim his aggression at Atticus- better that than at Mayella. Alexandra (rightly) suggests that Ewell may plot a secretive vengeance. Atticus (wrongly) says that no-one in Maycomb can keep anything secret.

On the legal implications of the case, **Atticus tells Jem that there will be an appeal, which may order a retrial, and is likely to acquit Tom (recognising that there is a miscarriage of justice).** Rape carries the death penalty in Alabama, but a jury could determine a long life sentence in prison instead. No jury in Alabama would commute a death sentence where the defendant is black.

Jem argues that there are two solutions to avoid the problem of wrongful conviction; rape should be made a less serious crime, and juries should be abolished.

Atticus (or, rather, Harper Lee) addresses this by saying it is right to make rape punishable by execution, but that the measure of proof- reasonable doubt- is weighted too much in favour of finding defendants guilty.

It is important to remember that the author's views are from a country where even today the death penalty remains in place. Because we live in the UK, where it is not, we are unlikely to agree with her views.

She believes that circumstantial evidence should not be enough to lead to a conviction; in the capital punishment type of case (like Tom's), a death sentence should be passed when there were one or two eye-witnesses to confirm the facts. Although it is Atticus who expresses these ideas, they are clearly the author's.

Her main thrust is on the rightness of raising the standard of evidence required for convicting, where there is a potential death sentence. Atticus says he would like to see the death penalty being determined only by judges, not by juries. But changing the law takes a long time- perhaps sixty or seventy years, for an issue like this.

To Jem's objection on juries- that, because they can make bad decisions, they should be abolished- **Atticus says that the problem is not the jury system, but racism**. Any form of discrimination on the grounds of race makes a white person "trash", and, if discrimination is allowed to continue, resentment will build, and social unrest will follow-

"it's all adding up and one of these days we're going to pay the bill for it. I hope it's not in you children's time."

This sounds, not so much like Atticus, but like the final speech of the Inspector in JB Priestley's "An Inspector Calls". In both cases, **the author is putting a social message into the mouth of a main character.**

Do you find it convincing?

Do you feel uncomfortable?

Personally, I resent finding such a blunt pronouncement in the middle of a piece of literature which is otherwise more pleasingly subtle.

The discussion then moves on to how juries are made up. Men are eligible, but women are not. And the men who make a living in the town are worried about the consequences of legal decisions they might have to make, so they have themselves excused from jury service.

In the case of Tom's jury, Atticus says, one of them- connected with the Cunninghams- wanted to acquit him, and had to be worn down by the others, who would not hear of it.

We are asked to accept that his change of attitude, from being part of the lynch mob to being a defender of Tom, is the result of the "considerable respect for the Finches" which came about when Scout took an interest in Walter Cunningham, and tried to have a conversation with him on his own terms.

The idea here is that **treating people fairly and without snobbery sets an example which they will themselves adopt, and this is how old prejudices and patterns of behaviour start to be broken down.** It would not have taken much more of this shift in thinking to have split the jury evenly- in which case Tom would have been found not guilty.

Scout, naturally, now wants to develop her alliance with Walter Cunningham junior- whose dignity she had defended in Chapter 2, before she brought him home for lunch in Chapter 3- as a way of accelerating this change. But Alexandra will not permit an invitation to Walter, because "they're not our kind of folks"; the social divide separates the Finches from the Cunninghams.

The point of this is that Harper Lee wants to drive home the idea that **racism is not so different from class or social snobbery.** It is easy to assume that some classes (or races) of people are inherently better than others. Alexandra's class-consciousness means that she says that, even if Walter Cunningham were a distant cousin of Scout's, he would not be invited to stay. We are reminded that at Finch Landing, Alexandra's home, Scout's cousin Francis Hancock revealed how early in life children in this community (apart from Atticus' children) become racists (see Chapter 9). Ironically, Francis absorbed his racist attitude from Alexandra herself. Scout remembers, too, that **Alexandra vetoed her invitation to visit Calpurnia at home- because such social visits imply a degree of equality which undermines and destabilises the racist status quo.**

Alexandra calls the Cunninghams "trash". We know the Ewells are trash. Atticus has said that any white person who exploits or discriminates against someone on racist grounds is trash. On that basis, **Alexandra is trash herself**.

Scout can distinguish, as her aunt does not, between the Cunninghams- whose loyalty and decency elevate them above the class-based and poverty-driven definition of "trash"- and the Ewells, who have no loyalty or decency, and are truly trash.

Jem tries to define the social strata of Maycomb County. He thinks that snobbery is the result of the length of time a family has been literate; Scout points out that literacy is learnt, and so the product of opportunity, not social superiority.

Jem finds it frustrating that people who share a common origin should be so argumentative and spiteful. He thinks, now, that Boo Radley may choose to remain alienated from Maycomb society. He is starting to understand that people can be hateful, both as individuals (Bob Ewell), groups (the jury) and communities (Maycomb as a whole).

Chapter 24

We now see the racism and (religious) hypocrisy of the ladies of Maycomb- in case there was any tendency on our part to suppose that it is just the male jury which is racist to its core.

Aunt Alexandra presides over a meeting of the missionary circle; it consists of eating cakes, drinking coffee, gossiping and moralising, first about the primitivism of the Mrunas, and then, inevitably, about their own servants.

The ladies make "soft bovine sounds" when they eat- they are like cattle; **easily led by the nose**. The air of self-satisfaction is shattered, briefly, when Atticus comes home to announce that **Tom has been shot (seventeen times) by his prison guards**. Only **Miss Maudie** Atkinson is clear about the real issues. She **is one of "the handful of people" (she says this phrase, pointedly, three times) who appreciate that Atticus is doing a necessary thing, in maintaining the values of inter-racial decency on behalf of the white community.**

There is an undertone, which the other ladies express through their conversation, that **dissatisfaction within the black community is becoming stronger. This reinforces the truth of Atticus' idea that there will be "a bill to pay" for discriminating against, and exploiting, black people**. Mrs Grace Merriweather, the arch-hypocrite, but who has not the faintest idea that she is herself one, says that the President's wife, Mrs Roosevelt, is mad to have come to Birmingham, Alabama and tried to sit with black people.

The chapter is set on the day before Dill leaves, at the end of the summer (as in Chapter 6). It is a Saturday. The formal part of the meeting takes up just the third paragraph- a report of a report (by

Mrs Grace Merriweather) on the "squalid" way of life of the Mruna tribe- whose habits are not that far removed from the Ewells.

The missionary circle has sent J Grimes Everett to bring them out of their "poverty.....darkness.....immorality....sin and squalor". Mrs Merriweather is the most devout lady in Maycomb. She has brown eyes, black hair, no children of her own, and she is readily moved to tearfulness when she relates the plight of the Mrunas.

Alexandra finally has her way, because Scout is dressed in her best clothes, can be showed off like a miniature lady, and helps Calpurnia; Alexandra "smiled brilliantly".

The Finch family are Methodists, but missionary circles are not exclusively denominational- so the neighbours come too (Miss Rachel Haverford, Miss Stephanie Crawford, and Miss Maudie, who, as we know, is a Baptist). Apart from Maudie, the others find Scout a figure of amusement.

Mrs Merriweather thinks that the church should tell Helen Robinson, whom she refers to as "that darky's wife", to "forgive and forget", and to lead a Christian life- in other words, **accept the death sentence.** She says that the black workers grumbled and sulked the day after the trial, and that the answer is for the white community to "let them know we forgive 'em"- **there is no doubt in her mind that Tom is guilty as charged.**

She is talking to Mrs Grace Farrow, "the second most devout lady in Maycomb", who has pale eyes, narrow feet, and tight grey ringlets. She **perpetuates the myth that black men are a sexual menace- "there's no lady safe in her bed these nights".** She makes a thinly veiled reference to **Atticus, as the main example of "good but misguided people", who are encouraging the black community to become sulky and dissatisfied.** She says that the northern states of America are hypocritical, because, having emancipated the slaves, they do not treat them as equals; in Alabama, segregation is an honest system ("we just say you live your way and we'll live ours").

Scout relates that Calpurnia has reported that, in prison, Tom has given up hope of being treated fairly. Atticus arrives unexpectedly, white-faced, to announce to her, Alexandra, Miss Maudie and Scout that **Tom is dead- shot (with unnecessary thoroughness) while trying to escape over the prison wall.** He would have escaped if he had been able-bodied, rather than handicapped by his damaged arm. Atticus takes it on himself to go and tell Helen Robinson what has happened.

Alexandra's reaction is to feel stress on behalf of Atticus, not grief for the Robinsons. She thinks that the people of Maycomb delegate to Atticus the worst and most unpleasant tasks, which they are too afraid to do themselves (such as defending Tom). Miss Maudie takes a more positive view; that **Atticus is the ambassador of the small number of people who are fair-minded and humane**, because they trust him always to do the right thing. **He is fighting a quiet campaign for humanity, and a minority of the population supports him.**

They go back to the room where the cakes are being eaten, and resume the gossip and small talk, ignoring- or not acknowledging- the fact of Tom's death. **The ladies are praising the missionary J Grimes Everett; they do not praise Atticus, who is doing much the same morally driven work in the community much closer to home.**

Chapter 25

The idea that Tom Robinson has been killed as a random act of violence is reinforced, in the opening lines, by the (apparently unconnected) discussion in which Jem tells Scout not to kill harmless insects; she should put them outside, or free them (as from prison) instead.

While Scout was at Aunt Alexandra's meeting, Jem had been teaching Dill to swim, and, when Atticus went past in the car on his way to see Helen Robinson, the boys had gone with him, but they were not allowed out of the car. Harper Lee inserts this into the narrative so that we can see the scene, as Dill related it to Scout- Helen simply collapsed in a shocked faint- and so that she can make the point that **Tom's violent death** causes only a momentary ripple on the calm pond (or swamp) of white Maycomb, and **serves to reinforce the racial stereotype that black people are impulsive, inclined to run away, and uncivilised.**

Mr Underwood writes an editorial in his paper, the Maycomb Tribune, which says **it is "a sin to kill cripples" and that shooting Tom is like "the senseless slaughter of songbirds". This reminds us of Atticus' key remark in Chapter 10 that "it's a sin to kill a mockingbird".** The remark about reprinting in The Montgomery Advertiser refers to its editor Grover Hall, whose campaigning had led to the collapse of the (racist) Ku Klux Klan in Alabama in about 1927. Atticus refers to this event in Chapter 15. Scout realises that, however properly the formalities of the trial were followed, it was a piece of hypocrisy, a charade, because there was never any possibility that Tom would be acquitted when accused of rape by a white woman.

Reports come back to Scout, via Miss Stephanie Crawford's gossip-mill, that Bob Ewell sees Tom's death as "one down and about two more to go". We do not know, yet, precisely what this means, but **Ewell wants to exact revenge on Judge Taylor and Atticus as well as the helpless Tom Robinson.**

Chapter 26

Scout starts her third school year, and walking past the Radleys' house brings back her memories of their attempts to communicate with Boo. The tree is still alive, despite the cement Mr Nathan Radley put into it. **Atticus warns her not to indulge her curiosity by going into the Radleys' garden, in case she is shot- which would be another over-zealous killing, like the shooting of Tom.**

Although Atticus is disapproved of, quietly, for his defence of Tom, he is still re-elected, without a contest, to the state legislature, because the people of Maycomb trust him to make the law.

At school, there is an initiative called Current Events, where children have to speak about a news story. Cecil Jacobs gives a half-digested account of Hitler's segregation, internment and persecution of the Jews. The teacher, **Miss Gates**, contrasts Hitler's dictatorial prejudice with American democracy, and **says- with unintended irony- that in America we don't believe in persecuting anybody. Tom Robinson is, of course, a symbol of the persecution of segregation; racism is America is no different from Hitler's oppression of the Jews, leading up to the Holocaust.** Cecil thinks that no-one who is white should be persecuted- which implies that other races can (and should) be.

Scout remembers that, on the way out of the trial, **the same Miss Gates had told Stephanie Crawford that the black community must be repressed, not integrated; that inter-racial marriage must not be allowed- that is, that racial segregation must be used to maintain the purity of American society.**

<u>**The same culture of racist thinking which Hitler is being accused of is in the DNA of the American education system.**</u>

Chapter 27

Bob Ewell's bitter resentment gathers force. He is given a job on the government's WPA scheme, but is- uniquely- sacked from it for being work-shy. But he mutters to the welfare officer he sees each week (when he signs on) that Atticus had him fired.

One Sunday evening, there is the suspicion of an attempted intruder at Judge Taylor's house.

Mr Link Deas creates a job for Helen Robinson as his cook, and perhaps at his shop; he seems to be unafraid of demonstrating a fair-minded attitude, rather like Atticus, and repaying loyalty with loyalty. When she is intimidated by Bob Ewell, and goes to work by a long way round, Deas walks past the Ewells' and shouts a warning that they are to leave her alone. Bob Ewell then stalks her, muttering obscenities. Deas confronts him and warns him off. **Bob Ewell threatening Helen with swear words is precisely what Mayella had accused Tom of, in Chapter 18.**

Alexandra and Atticus are still complacent about Ewell; they do not regard him as a threat, and he has not threatened them specifically.

In order to prevent practical jokes by the children of the town, a Halloween pageant, fayre, and costume competition is to be staged in the school hall. In the pageant (designed by Mrs Grace Merriweather) Scout is to be dressed up as a ham. Her costume is made of chicken wire with a painted cloth over it. She cannot get out of it without help; once in it, the capacity to move is very limited. It has peep-holes for eyes; in the next chapter, when she speaks, it sounds as though her voice is far away, because the cloth muffles it.

Atticus and Alexandra both make excuses for not going to the pageant- a device which enables Bob Ewell's assault to take place- and Alexandra has a premonition that something sinister is about to happen- she stops in mid-sentence, and explains that "somebody just walked over my grave". This is reminiscent of the children's discussion, in Chapter 4, of the supernatural.

Jem's offer to accompany Scout to the school commits them to what she obliquely refers to as "our longest journey together".

It is only on a second or third reading that we pick up the small details which connect our expectation of trouble with the threats of Bob Ewell; we expect them to be directed at Atticus himself, rather than at his children.

Chapter 28

As Scout and Jem walk to the school hall, **a solitary mockingbird is singing** in the Radleys' tree. There is no moon, and Scout trips on a tree root in the road. There is a landmark in the school yard-a large oak tree, which creates a cool shady spot. Jem has said (with what the reader can tell is accidental irony) that no-one will disturb the Radleys tonight- in fact, **this is the night Boo will finally come out** (to rescue him).

Cecil Jacobs jumps out and scares them; he is surprised that Atticus is not walking with them in the dark.

Because Scout falls asleep, makes her entrance late, and is told off by Mrs Merriweather, she will not leave until the audience has gone. She keeps her costume on (a mistake, but necessary for the dramatic climax). They are offered a lift home by an unidentified adult, and Jem refuses (another mistake, but necessary for the dramatic climax). Scout forgets her shoes, but the lights in the hall are switched off, so they cannot go back for them.

First Jem, then Scout, realises that **someone is following them (with hindsight, this is why Bob Ewell was reported to us as stalking Helen Robinson in chapter 27).** They think it is Cecil again, but there is a silence which he could not keep up. They can hear the person who is following them, shuffling and dragging his feet. Once they reach the oak tree (which is near the Radleys') it is a short distance to the road and the street-lamp; so, as they reach that cool spot, their attacker runs towards them.

As they start to run away, **Scout** trips, but **cannot get out of the wire costume (or "prison"- like Tom Robinson's prison).** Jem fights the attacker off and pulls Scout up. When they are almost at the road, he is pulled backwards and screams. **Then the attacker starts to strangle her, slowly (remember the marks on Mayella Ewell's neck, which her father had inflicted),** until he is himself thrown to the ground.

Scout realises that there is a fourth person under the tree- another man, who breathes heavily, coughs violently, and moves away unsteadily. As she reaches the road, she sees a man carrying Jem, whose left arm is dangling. She has found, on the ground, the body of a man who had been drinking whisky **(another clue – Bob Ewell spends his benefit money on whisky)** with something protruding between his waist and his chin- this turns out to be a kitchen knife.

Alexandra telephones for the doctor and Atticus phones for Heck Tate **(a parent whose child has been attacked should, unlike Bob Ewell, do both of these things)**. The man who rescued him and brought him home is standing in a corner; Scout has not seen him before. Heck returns, to state, at the end of the chapter, that Bob Ewell is under the tree, dead, stabbed with a kitchen knife.

Chapter 29

It is an odd place to break off for a new chapter; the conversation continues. Alexandra blames herself for not paying attention to her cold, chilling intuition of danger. But, as we know, she is as cold as Mount Everest herself!

Scout tells her version of events to Atticus and Heck Tate; Bob Ewell had attempted to kill her, as the knife had cut through the wire of her costume. Heck explains to Atticus that, emboldened by drink, Bob Ewell will dare to kill children; such vermin should be shot, not spoken to.

Scout's account repeats, very closely, the chase and scuffle, as it was presented in the previous chapter. This **only leaves the mystery man to be identified**; and his extreme pallor has left him with sickly white hands, the result of never being outside in the sun. At the very end of the chapter, Scout realises that it is Boo Radley, **and she addresses him, as she had dreamed of doing in Chapter 26.**

Chapter 30

Both Atticus and Dr Reynolds already know Arthur Radley by sight. As the doctor attends to Jem's arm, Atticus suggests they go on to the porch- Scout realises that Atticus fears that Arthur Radley may find the lights too strong inside the house. Scout guides him to a chair in the dark, and sits in the chair next to him.

Atticus assumes that Jem stabbed Bob Ewell in self-defence, and that the case will go to court; he sees events partly in terms of their legal consequences, with absolute respect for the law. **Heck asks him, twice, "Do you think (Jem killed Ewell)?"- almost exactly the wording of Atticus' key question, "Do you really think so?"** (see Chapter 15), which he asks Mr Link Deas, who is challenging the wisdom of Atticus accepting the job of defending Tom.

Heck says that Jem did not stab Ewell; Atticus takes this as a considerate plot to keep Jem out of court, and away from publicity, by hushing up the facts. Heck insists that Ewell "fell on his knife".

Atticus explains that, just as his need to maintain his self-respect meant he must defend Tom- because he could not expect his children to respect or obey him unless he lived conspicuously by the principles he always spoke about- so, now, for Jem to take his lead from him, he must undergo any legal investigation which is due.

"Losing" his children- he means losing their respect for him- is exactly what Atticus will not allow to happen. He says he must live in the same way in public and in private. This is precisely the integrity which Miss Maudie admires in him so much (see Chapter 5).

Heck Tate eventually has to be blunt with Atticus. It is not Jem he wants to protect from court proceedings; it is Arthur Radley. The knife he has in his pocket is a switchblade, which is the knife Ewell was carrying. The kitchen knife which killed Ewell, and which is still stuck in him, must, Heck says, be one Ewell found at the dump- but we realise that it is from the Radleys' kitchen.

Heck Tate says that **because Tom is dead and Ewell is responsible for his death, the right thing to do now is to "let the dead bury the dead"**- or, as we say today, let sleeping dogs lie. Heck knows that Arthur Radley was trying to prevent Ewell from murdering Jem and Scout; and that, if he is linked with their rescue, **the glare of publicity** (and cake) will be unbearable for him- it **would be a sin (like the sin to kill a mockingbird, as Scout reminds Atticus) to expose him to it.**

When the chapter ends with Atticus thanking Arthur Radley for protecting the children, we have almost forgotten he is there; **throughout the conversation which has ended with the decision to protect his privacy, Arthur Radley- the subject of the conversation- has not said a word.**

Chapter 31

Arthur Radley's terrible cough removes any last doubt we may have that he killed Bob Ewell, because it is the same cough Scout heard, under the tree, in the fight, in Chapter 28.

He is like a small child, apparently unable to speak, and with tentative and timid gestures; he strokes Jem's hair, at Scout's invitation, and holds her hand in a way which communicates when he wants to go home. **He asks Scout to take him home; he is asking her to protect him in the dark. After walking with him to his door, Scout never saw him again.**

After she has dropped him home, she pauses on Boo Radley's porch. The view from the Radleys' yard is different from that from her own porch.

Scout imagines the scene during the day, and herself and Jem running to meet Atticus as he walks home from his office; Jem with his fishing rod; Jem, Dill and her acting out their Radley drama; and a series of other memories, culminating in them somehow becoming, too, "Boo's children".

She is imagining the world as Boo has seen it over the years. *She now knows the meaning of Atticus' saying that you must think as if you are walking about in the shoes of the person whose mentality you are trying to understand.* More importantly, she can do it herself.

Scout finds Atticus sitting reading in Jem's room, while Jem sleeps, sedated; this is **exactly like the protection Atticus gave Tom on the night when he was in Maycomb jail** (see Chapter 15). She tries to stay awake, and he reads her the opening of "The Grey Ghost". She recites the plot in her sleep. The "ghost" is accused of crimes he had not committed, and, when seen by his accusers, is "real nice". So, **Scout and Jem were wrong to**

mythologise Boo Radley into a violent, scissors-wielding eater of cats and squirrels; and the whole community was wrong to demonise Tom Robinson as a rapist, and the black community as a whole.

Boo has turned out to be the grey ghost who has saved the children from Bob Ewell. In Chapter 1, Dill had bet this book, in his dare to make Jem touch the Radleys' house. Here, the book underlines the truth that people are often innocent of what they are accused of; Tom was innocent, and Boo is no malevolent phantom after all.

Atticus' approach to bringing up his children is justified. Knowing and **understanding the world is a matter of seeing people as they really are**, not as others do. He has always refused to hide them away from the harsh facts of Maycomb life, and they have survived (even if narrowly) - as he had hoped, at the end of Chapter 9- "without bitterness, and without catching Maycomb's usual disease".

Now for a quick reminder-

Especially at revision time, you may want to track which parts of the novel- which chapters, even- a particular character has an interesting or extended role in. You may also want to be clear about how much time passes between various points in the novel. If so, the short summaries here will give you that information.

Summary-Timeline & locations

Chapter 1: Summer 1933. Dill arrives. He, Jem and Scout are fascinated with Boo Radley's legend, and they try to make him come out of his house. Chapter is set in the Finch garden and the street. Brief appearance by Calpurnia.

Chapter 2: September 1933. Scout starts school; this is the first morning there. Other characters- Miss Fisher, Walter Cunningham.

Chapter 3: Lunchtime and the evening of the same day. At home- Scout and Atticus, and Calpurnia and Walter Cunningham. At school: an unpleasant introduction- for the reader- to Burris Ewell. Atticus agrees with Scout that they will continue reading at home.

Chapter 4: Summer 1934. Scout finds chewing-gum left in the Radleys' tree. It is the end of the school year. She and Jem find the two pennies (dated 1900 and 1906) in a jewel-box, in the tree. Two days later, Dill arrives. They roll the tyre, and invent the stage play of the Radleys, which becomes more elaborate as the summer holidays pass.

Chapter 5: A composite version of some of the evening discussions between Scout and Miss Maudie. Dill, Jem and Scout launch the raid on the Radleys' house, with their letter to Boo, but Atticus catches them in the act.

Chapter 6:   September 1934, the last night of Dill's stay. Dill, Jem and Scout invade the Radleys' back garden so that the boys can look in through the window. Jem has to go back later, to retrieve his trousers which have been mended, mysteriously.

Chapter 7:   A week later; the start of Scout's second school year. In October, on four occasions three weeks apart, they find gifts in the tree. When Scout and Jem go to leave a note, they find that Nathan Radley has concreted the hole in the tree.

Chapter 8:   On an unspecified day that winter it snows, for the first time since 1885. Scout and Jem make a snowman. That night, Miss Maudie's house burns down. Atticus and Miss Maudie feature here.

Chapter 9:   Cecil Jacobs uses the slur that "Atticus defends niggers" at school. Scout and Atticus discuss it; she walks away from a fight a school the next day. Christmas Eve- Uncle Jack arrives at Maycomb. Christmas Day away at Finch Landing (with Alexandra, and Francis Hancock). Back at home- discussions between Jack and Scout and Atticus.

Chapter 10:   Talk about the trial starts at school. Scout and Miss Maudie discuss Atticus' skills. One Saturday (in February 1935) the mad dog, Tim Johnson, appears; Heck Tate asks Atticus to shoot it.

Chapter 11:   The children are now in the habit of walking to the shops, and they have to pass Mrs Dubose, who lives two doors up. One of these trips is on the day after Jem's twelfth birthday- in 1935- a Saturday- and Mrs Dubose says that Atticus is as bad as "the niggers and trash he works for". Jem vandalises her garden, and, that evening, Atticus sends him back to talk with her. He comes back with the mission to read to her for a month. The first session takes place the following Monday; the month is extended by a week, and then Mrs Dubose dies.

You will see from this summary that **Part One of the novel really does reflect the narrow horizons and small territory Scout occupies; her own house and garden, the neighbours', the street, and (in small parts) school; and Finch Landing.**

Just as there is a small and familiar set of locations, there is a small and familiar set of characters. This is realistic, because Scout is only seven, then eight- not, of course, that the novel is written in the style of an eight-year-old!

Part 2 will not take us much further afield, geographically, but what Scouts sees, outside and inside the courthouse, and at Calpurnia's church, will be much more educational than school. Then the attack by Bob Ewell brings danger much closer to home than anyone expected. And the unseen neighbour- Boo- finally appears, to complete the society of neighbours and lay to rest the fantasies of childhood.

Chapter 12: Jem is now aged 12. It is summer 1935- a few weeks after Mrs Dubose has died- but Dill writes to say that he cannot come. Atticus is called away for two weeks for an emergency session of the state legislature. Calpurnia takes Scout and Jem to her church, where we meet Rev Sykes and Zeebo (Calpurnia's son, and the town rubbish collector).

Chapter 13: Later that day (Sunday) Alexandra comes to stay; Atticus returns from his business trip to Montgomery. The first month of Alexandra's stay passes. She sends Atticus to tell the children about their family's "gentle breeding"- a pretentious and snobbish idea which Atticus tells them to forget about.

Chapter 14: There is a quiet whisper of disapproval now when Scout and Jem go to the shops on Saturdays, because Tom's trial is nearer. Alexandra forbids Scout from visiting Calpurnia at her home. Dill is hiding under Scout's bed, after running away from his "new father". He is allowed to stay the night.

Chapter 15: Dill stays. A week later, Heck Tate and a group of men alert Atticus to the fact that Tom Robinson is to be held in the Maycomb jail the following day (Sunday) in anticipation of his trial starting on Monday. On the Sunday morning, Atticus has another discussion with Heck and others about the potential for a mob to take the law into its own hands, deny Tom any trial, and lynch him. That evening, Atticus leaves the house and drives the half-mile to the town square with his extension lead and light bulb, and a chair- to guard Tom. Just before 10pm, the children follow. Scout defuses the confrontation with the rural lynch mob from Old

Sarum. These men will more or less make up the jury at the trial, too.

Chapter 16:   The same Sunday night, then Monday morning. Scout is nearly nine years old. The trial starts, with the jury being selected in the morning. The trial begins in the afternoon, with Heck Tate giving evidence. Meanwhile, we have a more detailed understanding of Dolphus Raymond and of Judge Taylor.

Chapter 17:   The evidence of Heck Tate and Bob Ewell. The state prosecutor has very few questions; he is doing the bare minimum, partly because he is relying on the usual outcome in a racial trial, and partly because there is little he can do to undermine Atticus' line of questioning and his conclusions. According to Mr Underwood, the children took their seats at 1.18pm.

Chapter 18:   Mayella gives her "evidence", after which there is a ten minute recess. It is then almost 4pm, and the judge suggests that, as the defence has only one witness- the accused- Atticus should give the defence case, because the trial should be able to finish in the one day.

Chapter 19:   Atticus helps Tom Robinson to put the defence case; Mayella is "mistaken in her mind"; everyone can see that his left hand is of no use to him, so it cannot be him who punched Mayella. After part of the evidence, Dill is crying, so Scout takes him outside.

Chapter 20: Atticus is summing up to the jury; Jem has heard the five minutes of this which Scout has missed. The rest of this chapter cannot take up more than ten minutes.

Chapter 21: Having gone home for a meal, the children are back less than an hour later. The jury has been "out" (considering its verdict) for about half an hour, after being spoken to by Mr Gilmer and being given instructions by Judge Taylor. The time goes on from before 8pm until after 11pm; some time after this, the jury returns, with its guilty verdict. Chapters 17-21 have dealt with a single day- the day of the trial. They make up one sixth of the whole novel.

Chapter 22: Atticus explains to Jem that this is not the first case of racially motivated injustice; nor will it be the last. The following morning, he reminds Jem that there will be an appeal against the verdict. Jem tells Miss Maudie that he has lost his faith in the goodness of the people of the area.

Chapter 23: Atticus, Jem, Scout and Alexandra discuss the threat Bob Ewell has made; the faults with the justice system; and Alexandra's views on who the children should associate with (not Calpurnia and not the Cunninghams)

Chapter 24: Alexandra hosts the meeting of the ladies' missionary society; Mrs Farrow and Mrs Merriweather exhibit snobbish, hypocritical and racist attitudes. Miss Maudie expresses her appreciation of Atticus, when he returns with the news that

Tom has been shot. The five chapters of the trial in the courtroom have been balanced by three chapters set in the Finch household.

Chapter 25: Atticus goes to the Quarters to tell Helen Robinson that Tom is dead. His shooting makes the news for two days. The following week, Mr Underwood uses the Maycomb Tribune to argue that Tom's death is "senseless slaughter".

Chapter 26: September 1935. School resumes; Scout is in the third grade, and Jem the seventh, so he goes to the high school, not the grammar school. Scout has her "current events" lesson at school, with Miss Gates claiming that in America "we don't believe in persecuting anybody" (unlike Hitler's ethnic cleansing of the Jews). Scout remembers the hateful comments Miss Gates had made as she left the trial. Jem's adolescent need for justice makes him a touchy teenager now.

Chapter 27: In Mid-October 1935, Bob Ewell loses his WPA job almost as soon as he starts it, and he repeats his threats. He is the unnamed intruder at Judge Taylor's house, and he stalks and insults Helen Robinson. The chapter ends with Scout dressing in her ham costume for the pageant; it is the evening of Hallowe'en, 31st October 1935.

Chapter 28: Scout and Jem walk to school for the pageant; they are attacked in the dark on the way home. Jem's as yet unidentified rescuer (Boo Radley) carries him home. Dr Reynolds and Heck Tate are called. Bob Ewell is dead under the tree.

Chapter 29:   Sheriff Heck Tate effectively takes a witness statement from Scout- her account of the attack- and Boo is identified, standing in the corner, and leaning against the wall.

Chapter 30:   Atticus, Heck Tate, Scout and Boo go out on to the porch to discuss the presentation of Ewell's death .Atticus assumes Jem killed him, and should not be protected from a charge of murder (in self-defence). Heck knows that Boo killed him, and he believes that he deserves to be kept out of the public eye, after providing a public service, in getting rid of Bob Ewell.

Chapter 31:   Boo says goodbye to Jem and Scout, goes home, and disappears inside for ever ("I never saw him again"). The novel ends with Jem and Scout asleep, and Atticus confirming that, as with Boo, whose gossiped about mythical personality bears no resemblance to his true self, "most people are....real nice....when you finally see them". Atticus is really referring to the African American community.

Part Two of the novel takes place between June or July and 31st October 1935. Having witnessed Tom Robinson's trial, the perversion of justice, the hypocrisy of most of the people of Maycomb, and Bob Ewell's vindictive attempts at revenge, Scout reflects that there is nothing much to be learned at school "except possibly algebra".

Maycomb really has only one thing to teach its children- the nature of prejudice, and the need to eradicate it. The trouble of course, is that these are lessons its adults need to learn too.

Understanding the meaning of the novel as a whole

The novel opens with the comment that **"people moved slowly"** in Maycomb. This is partly because the climate is hot, but it is also **a measure of their attitudes**. Atticus knows, from before he even starts defending Tom, that the case is a lost cause. Everyone except Atticus and his children (and Dill) believes that segregation is justified, and/or a fact of life; nobody questions its basis.

Aunt Alexandra embodies the fossilised, backward-looking thinking which dominates the white community. Her son, Francis Hancock develops his casual racism from her (Chapter 9). She never understands why Atticus agreed to accept Tom's case (she does not understand concepts of integrity and conscience), and she believes that his accepting it will damage the family's reputation, because it will bring **shame** on them. She believes that society should be preserved as it is, with the characteristics and behaviours of all the old families settled and recognisable. She disapproves of informality, and tries to make Scout lady-like, and to insulate her and Jem from the real world.

Harper Lee wants to show us that **white society is hypocritical**; Maycomb believes that, behind the **"thin veneer"** (to borrow the phrase used in chapter 25) of the surface, civilisation, in the black community, is only skin deep, because they are **primitive savages** underneath the surface.

His own sister Alexandra exhibits precisely the **indiscriminate discrimination** which Atticus is so scathing about when he sums up at the trial at the end of Chapter 20. These things can only be said in court; and, even there, they are ignored. A jury has its collective identity and its members can avoid taking personal responsibility for its decisions.

The ladies' missionary society sponsors the missionary J Grimes Everitt, who is trying to "make Christians" of the Mruna tribe. The question is whether this is desirable, considering the type of Christians Mrs Merriweather and Mrs Farrow- the two most devout women in Maycomb- are. **Mrs Farrow thinks that all African American men are potential rapists** (Chapter 24) and Mrs Merriweather tells her servant Sophy that "being a Christian" means accepting her subservient position cheerfully, and being grateful for low-paid employment, with no thought of questioning your own inferiority.

At the end of Chapter 26, Scout remembers that, on the way out of the trial, her teacher, Miss Gates, had said that the black community **"were getting' way above themselves, an' the next thing they think they can do is marry us".** **In the opening chapter, we are told that the white community is inbred- Atticus "was related by blood or marriage to nearly every family in the town". The absence of newcomers to the town means it is stuck in a vicious cycle of insular, unthinking prejudice.**

This irrational **terror** of social equality- based on an underlying, embedded prejudice that black people are all savages under the skin, and a deep-seated fear that their sexuality is threatening and dangerous- helps us to see why **Tom was a condemned man from the moment Mayella Ewell screamed**, why he could not push her out of the way, in order to escape, and why the subversive **idea that a white girl could make sexual advances to a black man must be blotted out, because it is simply unthinkable.**

The (to us, in 2015, obvious) point that racism has no justifiable basis is made, not just through the attitudes and behaviour of Atticus (backed up by his fan and supporter, Miss Maudie Atkinson), but in subtler ways. When Jem and Scout visit

Calpurnia's church in Chapter 12, they are welcomed by all except the morally defective Lula, who believes in racial (and religious) segregation- "they got our church, we got our'n"- and in part because of those views is an outsider in her own society.

When we compare Chapter 12 with Chapter 24, we can see that, in Maycomb, racism is compatible with religious belief, even for those who see themselves as righteous. **Which church would you prefer to be a member of**- First Purchase M.E Church, or the Maycomb Alabama Methodist Episcopal Church South? As Calpurnia says, it's all the same God; but it is certainly not all the same society.

The children have picked up a sense of the fundamental absurdity of racism, because Uncle Jack has discussed with them the common origin of the human race, in Africa (Chapter 16). At the end of Chapter 23, Scout tells Jem that Atticus believes that **every family shares the same origins and ancestry, regardless of their eventual colour or what part of the world they happen to live in now**.

It is not an accident that **the way Jem is injured**- his broken elbow means that his left arm is shorter than his right- **is so similar to Tom Robinson's childhood disfigurement; it is a memorial to it**.

Jem, like Tom, will become an upright young man, but he will not be condemned to death for an imaginary crime, simply because of the colour of his skin. **Just as the snowman in Chapter 8 is mud-based, and only white because it has a skin of snow, the exterior or surface of human beings cannot disguise the fact that, underneath, everyone is fundamentally the same. The various discussions about breeding (or trash), and about "background", highlight the difference between the child's (unprejudiced) view and the adults' (biased) perspective.**

Atticus' uniqueness lies partly in his lack of interest in worthless social attitudes and conventions. His **children**, therefore, question what they see, instead of accepting it automatically.They **work from the principle of equality, where the majority of the adults in Maycomb start from the principle of inequality**. Atticus will **defend whoever and whatever deserves to be defended** (Tom; the legal system; Scout's entitlement to read at home; the Radleys' right to privacy; his children's need to be exposed to the unfairness and faults of the world they live in; education in its widest sense; fairness).

How important is the theme of "growing up", and the attention given to the emotional development of Scout and Jem during the course of the novel? Children can have a degree of innocence and idealism in the way they see issues, which we might regard as simplistic in an adult character. **Scout is a mini Miss Maudie, and Jem is a mini Atticus.** The frustration and angry disappointment which Jem demonstrates at the miscarriage of justice is really there to reflect our feelings (and Atticus', which, with typical self-control and dignity, he keeps to himself).

I don't agree with the idea that the novel is a *Bildungsroman* or coming-of-age story. How can it be, when Scout is still a child and Jem barely a teenager at the end?

"To Kill a Mockingbird" is, rather, a novel about personal morality and justice in the social sense, as well as the legal one.

Whereas, in, for example, "Jane Eyre" or "Great Expectations", we follow the protagonist's journey from childhood to the maturity of an adult, **Harper Lee uses the child's eye view- throughout- to engage our perceptions about fairness, hypocrisy and prejudice**- not so much in order to show the protagonists put them aside, as to show us how deeply rooted they are in a society like Maycomb.

As deeply rooted, and as damaging, in fact, as the nutgrass Miss Maudie persecutes in Chapter 5.

In the coming-of-age novel, the protagonist learns to modify his childhood ideas in the light of experiencing the adult world. **Scout and Jem do not need to change their views; their beliefs are the same as Atticus', and are right.**

They need to hold on to those beliefs, but develop an Atticus-type detachment, instead of being upset, when they lose a small skirmish in the long campaign for equality.

Moreover, in the coming-of-age novel, the hero/heroine learns from the antagonist who becomes their friend or ally; Jane Eyre learns from Rochester (and vice versa), and Pip Pirrip learns from the unyielding Estella. If the children, Scout and Jem- and particularly Scout- are the protagonists in our novel, who is their antagonist? Not Boo Radley! Not Aunt Alexandra. Not even Mrs Dubose, Cecil Jacobs or Bob Ewell. **Their antagonist is Maycomb itself**.

Sample essays

Essay technique is a vital part of your armoury when you're fighting for good grades in your exams. It's easy to learn, and to practice; *it's also very easy to underperform, and do yourself less than justice, by ignoring it.*

If you were a professional sportsman or woman, or a professional musician, and your living depended on your results, you would make sure you practise your skills, every day, so that they are sharp and familiar to you, whenever you need them.

Essay writing needs to become a skill in exactly the same way-
because your future income and prospects may be affected by
your exam grades.

Really.

The exam essays we're dealing with require you to do things-

-understand the question

-plan and organise your answer

-write clearly and correctly

Under the pressure of a real exam, many people just panic. They
don't read the question properly, or they misread it, or they answer
the question they wish had been set, or they start writing in the
quotations they've learnt, whether they are relevant or not.

At least as many candidates then decide not to make a plan- even
though the exam paper will say that planning time has been
allowed for, in allowing you, for example, 45 minutes to answer
this question.

The answer booklet is full of blank pages. For some people, the
challenge seems to be to fill all those pages- with quantity, not
quality. If you stick to the question, follow through and develop
each of your points, from your plan, and write a short conclusion,
then less can in fact be more!

What happens if you don't plan?

Your essay will wander off the subject of the question. And you won't know when you've finished your answer. So you may be tempted to write a bit more…..and some more….and then you run out of time for the rest of the paper, and throw away handfuls of marks. Just through being disorganised. You can avoid this! You simply need to practise properly beforehand, and stay focused in the exam itself.

How this study guide makes it simple to do well

"To Kill a Mockingbird" has 31 chapters. This guide will help you to be very familiar with the plot, the characters, and the timeline of the novel. There is also a list for you of who is in which chapter, so that, if you are practicing by preparing an essay on a particular character, you can refer to the chapters where they have a role easily and quickly.

Also, I have used **bold type** in the chapter analyses, to show you where ideas or themes recur. I have identified important motifs and commented on them. This guide is designed to help you find your way round the novel, so that you can turn to the relevant material whenever you need to. I aim to save you a good deal of revision time you'd otherwise be using thumbing backwards and forwards through the novel.

Your **essay plan** will be on a **single piece of paper**. It will gather together all the material you will be using to answer the question. Just use a word or phrase, and don't write your point out fully until you write your answer. Then when you write your essay you can write these points out in whole sentences and paragraphs.

You must use your material in a way that shows **why it is relevant** and what it contributes. Short references and quotations will help here. Do not fill your answer with quotes! Exams today are not about memorising chunks of text (you will have the book with you anyhow, with most exam boards). Too many quotations generally means not enough analysis and too little evidence that you have a view or response of your own.

Your **plan** will need to have perhaps **seven or eight points** in it.

Your opening should not be of the uncertain "I am going to write about......" variety. That sounds like a tired old car engine struggling to start on a cold winter morning. **Make your opening sentence or two a clear statement of your point of view**. This will keep you on track.

Then **prioritise your points**, and use the most important ones first. Why? Because if you run out of time you will have made your most important points; and your most important points will be the most interesting ones for a marker to read.

Applying what you know

Now, we're going to take this method and use it to create answers to three essay questions. See whether you agree with me that this is a guaranteed way to get the most out of your ideas, and manage your time in the exam to maximise your marks.

Sample Essay 1

In chapter 20, Atticus tells the jury "this case is as simple as black and white". How far do you agree with him, and why?

Plan

The evidence in the trial is simple, but Tom found guilty. Why? Legal facts vs fears, attitudes, cultural racism and prejudices- how easy to shift? Adults/children- attitudes, flexibility- case hopeless. Lynch mob. Atticus' role in community and as parent. Rational motives/ other people's irrational motives. Scottsboro Case. TKAM- historic significance and meaning.

Answer

As a lawyer, Atticus can and does show that Tom Robinson could not have committed the crime he is accused of; with a damaged left arm, he could not have beaten Mayella Ewell, and Atticus shows that both she and her father are lying about what really happened.

This should be enough; but the jury still finds Tom guilty of rape, because the word of an African American will never be accepted, in Maycomb in 1935, over the word of a white trash father and his daughter. In the legal sense, the case is black and white, both in the racial sense, and in the sense that it is open and shut. Yet Atticus knows that he will lose it before he even takes it on. He judges his success by the small triumph of making the jury deliberate for some time, instead of ignoring the evidence altogether. His defence of Tom makes it impossible for the jury to resort to the usual blind prejudice; the members of the jury have to pause before they return the automatic verdict of "guilty". This is the first step on the long road to civil rights, fairness and equality, which, as Atticus says, should be guaranteed to every defendant in the courtroom, but is not.

The lynch mob which assembles outside the Maycomb jail in Chapter 15 means to hang Tom without even the charade of a trial. It is only Scout's resourcefulness which turns them away. If Tom had been white, this ugly threat would not exist.

At the end of Chapter 26, Scout remembers that her teacher, Miss Gates, had left the court ridiculing the idea of inter-racial marriage. And in Chapter 24 Mrs Farrow says that "there's no lady safe in her bed"- alluding to the irrational fear (on the part of "Southern womanhood") that all African Americans are potential rapists. Atticus tells the jury, in Chapter 20, "some Negro men are not to be trusted around women". But the same thing is true of any race, and of the whole "human race". Bob Ewell is not to be trusted around his own daughter Mayella, whom he abuses.

Tom is found guilty purely because of racial prejudice. This is a disease mainly of adults- Scout, Jem and Dill cannot understand the concept of racial segregation. Dolphus Raymond prefers to live in the African American community, and his children are of mixed race; but, to avoid confrontation, he acts as if he is an addled alcoholic. Atticus' own sister, Alexandra, is a racist. She disapproves of Atticus' agreeing to defend Tom- she thinks it brings shame on the family- and she passes her prejudices on to her grandson, Francis Hancock (Chapter 9). Scout's classmate, Cecil Jacobs, is equally prejudiced. Of the adults, only Miss Maudie has the decency to stay away from the court, describing it as a "Roman carnival" (Chapter 16) - a spectacle in which helpless slaves or Christians would be fed to the lions for the entertainment of a savage, bloodthirsty public mob.

She explains to Scout the important truth that Atticus has a degree of integrity and morality which sets him above the herd (Chapter 5- "Atticus Finch is the same in his house as he is on the public streets"). She tells Alexandra (Chapter 24) that "we trust him to do right". This explains why, although the white community thinks that Tom does not deserve a competent legal defence, Atticus will still be elected unopposed to the state legislature as the county's lawyer- an election which is made only by white citizens.

Atticus is chosen by Judge Taylor to give Tom the quality of defence he would not be given by the junior barrister Maxwell Green (Chapter 22), in order to push Maycomb "a baby-step" towards fairness. Atticus takes the case because, if he did not, he would have no authority with Scout and Jem (because he would have been a coward and not been prepared to defend principles that he is trying to instil in them). He shows them the bravery of Mrs Dubose in a losing cause (death from cancer); Tom's trial will be equally hopeless; but his children must understand the meaning of courage, which is to stand up for what is right, whether that means resisting the lynch mob, or standing up for the rights of a minority or underclass which is cheated by "trash" like Bob Ewell.

Atticus cannot tell his children to treat everyone else impartially unless he can demonstrate that he lives his own life in just that way. He cannot expect them to fight for equality, without losing hope, if he has not set the same brave example.

In Chapter 23, he tells Jem that the jury is made up of "twelve reasonable men in ordinary life"; but that they lose their capacity to be fair when they try a black defendant, because of the prejudices of the community which they have always lived in. This is why he has warned the children, in Chapter 9, that "no matter how bitter things get, they're still our friends". Change and tolerance can only develop from within the community; trying to impose a lack of prejudice on the people of Maycomb is as difficult as trying to convert the (fictional) Mruna tribe to Christianity in Chapter 24.

Maycomb is a fictional version of Harper Lee's home town of Monroeville, Alabama; it was right at the heart of the civil rights movement which emerged, with Martin Luther King leading it, from the Alabama bus boycott in 1956. It was also the landscape of the Scottsboro trials (from 1931), in which discredited allegations of rape by discredited accusers were upheld against African American youths. Harper Lee is saying that, just as Atticus stood up for the oppressed Tom Robinson in 1935, her reading public in the years from 1960 must take sides, and align themselves with the call for fairness, and an end to the segregation which went back at least as far as the Alabama code of 1901. That legal code sits, unused, in Atticus' office, because the law, in itself, cannot resist or eliminate prejudice. Harper Lee challenges us all, as her readers, to make the necessary "baby-steps" to end racism and all its injustices.

Atticus is right to say that Tom's case is simple; the evidence proves his innocence. But, in the context of this novel, the phrase "black and white" also refers- ironically- to the complexity, and the complex, of irrationality (Maycomb's "usual disease") which means that the best lawyer in the world cannot (yet) defend Tom against racist hatred. The racial issue both complicates and simplifies the trial.

Maycomb's school education is as bad as its teachers, and its law is as bad as its juries. Changing the fundamental, inbred, slow, unintelligent, superstitious way of thinking which settles for this is anything but simple.

It is, indeed, a case of black and white, but it is a very difficult case, or challenge, to disprove what has always been accepted without contest, and to question, and to start again. The challenge demands the innate sense of equality, in our view of the world, which only the idealistic child- Jem, Scout, Dill- is likely to be able to bring to the ugly world of Maycomb.

So, Atticus says (Chapter 16) that Maycomb needs "a police force of children"- because, in Maycomb, you have to be like a child, in order to stand in the shoes of someone who takes a different view, and find a peaceful way to replace prejudice with fairness.

Sample Essay 2

Explain why Boo Radley is important in the novel.

Plan

 Boo not seen; stories; children's games; heard laughing. Gifts in tree. Rescues Jem and Scout. Go on trial? Atticus/ Heck Tate. Perception and truth. Savage or civilised? Parallels with Tom. Mockingbirds. Scout's view from his porch.

Answer

Boo Radley is an important presence in the novel because, when he is not outside his house, to defend himself, all sorts of allegations are made about him- and believed. Much the same could be said of Tom Robinson; except that Tom is not believed in public either. Both men have a certain vulnerability, and some child-like characteristics. Both are demonised by the white community they live in. Only Boo has the opportunity to restore his reputation.

Dill invents a history for Boo- that he is a nocturnal prowler who looks in at people's windows (this is a version of the fear or rape complex which was used by adults to justify the lynch mobs); and that he eats cats and squirrels. He is not really a "malevolent phantom", but a child trapped in a man's body. The key clue is the laughter Scout hears when the tyre rolls up to the Radleys' house; but Boo mends Jem's trousers (clumsily), and leaves the various gifts in the knot-hole of the tree- actions which show he wants to play with them, or interact with them on a child to child basis. Nathan Radley fills the hole because he does not want Boo to have any contact with other families. This may be to do with Boo's probable mental illness, or it may be to do with his strict Baptist beliefs.

Boo's behaviour undermines the idea that he is evil; and when he rescues Jem and Scout, and kills Bob Ewell, he risks becoming a mockingbird, in the sense that he would be unable to cope with public attention or acclaim. For Heck Tate, the injustice done to Tom Robinson is enough; Boo must be protected, as a harmless songbird, from being "shot at" (by cameras?).

Bob Ewell has destroyed Tom Robinson; Mr Tate does not want Ewell (even now that he is dead) to be able to do the same to Boo, who would run the risk of being found guilty of murder, or, more probably, become a celebrity for saving the Finch children.

It is only at the end of the novel that Boo can reveal himself; in the meantime, a life story has been invented for him, by other people. The assumption, in Maycomb, is that if you are unfriendly (or too friendly) there must be something wrong with you. Where Boo is unsociable, Tom is too friendly- in helping Mayella Ewell, and feeling sorry for her. The jury, and most of Maycomb, assumes that Tom is a rapist, because all black men must be; and that the word of two trashy Ewells is worth more than that of the "humble, respectable" Tom, because they are white and he is not. Tom is as harmless as Boo (and as a mockingbird) because of his disability and his polite disposition. When he is shot, only his own family is affected for long. Mr Underwood's editorials are soon forgotten too. There is a grim irony, in that Boo (a mockingbird) strikes back, and kills the killer of Tom (as we must adjudge Bob Ewell)- the revenge of the Ewells becomes the revenge of the mockingbirds.

Boo and Tom both have a dark event in their past- Boo's stabbing his father, and Tom's 30 days in prison for fighting. The children assume that this makes Boo dangerous and unstable, as the jury thinks Tom is; both are wrong. Atticus' key dogma applies here- you can only understand someone else when you inhabit their skin and walk around in it. At the end of the novel, Scout stands on Boo's porch and does precisely that. She can sense how simple and childlike Boo is, and how wrong they were to let their wild imaginations invent a character for him. The tragedy is that the jury allowed its fiction of Tom to be the defendant it judged- not Tom himself.

The end of the novel brings Atticus and Boo together; the children are, somehow, Boo's, as well as Atticus', because he has helped to protect them. Atticus' main recreation is reading the local papers; it seems that Boo does the same. They share the mission to keep the Finch children safe from harm. Atticus killed the mad dog, and Boo killed the mad Bob Ewell (whom Heck Tate calls a skunk, or vermin).

Atticus' public profile means that everyone respects him, even if they disapprove of "lawing for niggers". Boo is so private that he has no respect in the community he inhabits, and neither does Tom- because of pure racism. Both men are demonised; they are victims of a taboo or superstition about their unfitness to play a full part in society.

In one sense, Boo's "coming out" marks the end of Scout's childish imaginings. Although she falls asleep to Atticus' reading of "the Grey Ghost", the world of boys' adventure literature is less of a focus for her now; she has seen how friendship (Walter

Cunningham) can help to defuse or avoid conflict; she has witnessed the bravery, of Mrs Dubose, of her father (in taking on a hopeless cause), and of Boo. There are real dangers and real prejudices; real battles to be fought, not with fists, but with the moral power of the need for equality. The influence of Calpurnia and Miss Maudie will make Scout a reformer. Boo's role in her formative years has been to prove the gap between perception and reality, and to validate her father's demands for tolerance and open-mindedness. If Scout's generation can make those values the norm instead of the exception, then fairness, equality and desegregation will follow eventually.

Jem and Scout both become more knowing about the world of Maycomb, and less innocent. The theme of innocence (or naivete) runs through the grouping of the children plus Tom plus Boo. Boo's older brother rebuffs the children's attempts to engage and befriend Boo. The court punishes Tom for his innocent instinct to help Mayella because he feels sorry for her (the unspeakable truth is that she is even more abused and excluded, socially, than a black person).

Boo observes, from inside his domestic prison, the innocent friendship among the three children which he has been denied for the past 15 years. By leaving the gifts in the tree, and putting the blanket over Scout on the night of the fire, he exhibits the same care and concern which Atticus shows towards the Robinson family.

We can only try to imagine how difficult it is for Boo, with what Heck Tate calls "his shy ways", to come out and risk his own life to save the children. In not allowing the innocent and vulnerable to be attacked without an adult to defend them, Boo demonstrates the same morality and courage as Atticus, in defending Tom, regardless of the personal danger it puts him in.

The very end of the novel aligns the children's story title "the Grey Ghost" with Boo, who had been grey and ghostly throughout, and with Atticus' observation that, when you "finally see" people as they really are- not as you think they are- most are "real nice". Boo's invisibility (as a white man), and the lack of compassion extended to him, is similar to the experience of the black Tom Robinson. Jem's snowman- mud-coloured on the inside, and white only on the surface- reminds us that social exclusion and prejudice are not exclusively linked with racism.

Boo Radley confounds the prejudices about him, and shows himself as a surrogate father/protector, while he is also, in many ways, a child. The parallels with other victims/outsiders (Tom) and other prejudices (racism) give Boo a symbolic value which adds to the depth of the meaning of the novel. It would not be the same without him.

Sample Essay 3

"Scout and Jem are unconvincing for their ages". To what extent to you agree with this, and why does it matter?

Plan

Need to be young in order to question racism; assume the world should be unbiased; be an easy target; represent the need for flexible thinking; allow the criticism of the school system; accept what Atticus tells them.

Need to be mature characters in order to- be outraged by injustice; see where fault lies; disarm the lynch mob.

Answer

At the start of the novel, Scout is almost six and Jem is almost ten. The first sentence, strangely perhaps, tells us how old the children are by the time the book ends. By then, Jem will be almost thirteen (and will have just broken his arm) and Scout will be almost nine.

Although the narrative is told from Scout's perspective, Jem is an important figure. During the course of the book, he becomes less child-like and less interested in games and tree-houses, and more concerned about right and wrong (track his responses to the evidence given at the trial), and playing American football. His frustration with Atticus (who is too old and visually impaired for contact sports) is milder, once he realises that his father is such a gifted marksman. He refuses to go home, when the mob threatens Atticus; Atticus is not authoritarian by nature, and, although he believes that it is wrong to try to immunise his children against the ugly reality of the world outside their door, Jem starts to push the boundaries, and assert his own independence of judgment.

Jem exhibits a combination of idealism, about the need to reform the legal/justice system, and alienation and moodiness- all recognisable adolescent attributes, but perhaps more characteristic of teenagers than pre-teens. His ambivalence about emulating Atticus, and becoming a lawyer, is authentic- we tend to look up to our parents, while we also find fault with some of their decisions, which we regard as flawed or incomprehensible.

His injury, at the hands of Bob Ewell, leaves Jem with (and as) a visible reminder of Tom Robinson, whose left arm was damaged to a similar extent. It also arises from protecting Scout against the evil Ewell; a parallel with Atticus' defence of Tom in court.

"Scout" tells the story of the novel with a degree of detail and a range of language which only an adult has available to them. Her extreme youth is critically useful when she persists in trying to engage Walter Cunningham Snr in a conversation about his legal affairs and her friendship with his son. Atticus judges that she has averted the violence the lynch mob would have done to him, and defused the confrontation, by making Cunningham see a different point of view.

Younger children will have no natural inbuilt bias towards racism (although Francis Hancock and Cecil Jacobs have both picked the "disease" up). Scout and Jem (and Dill) discuss the basis for racism, first of all in an importantly positioned passage in Chapter 16- immediately before the start of the trial- and in Chapter 23. In Chapter 12, Jem wants to run away from the discomfort he feels when Lula expresses an anti-white prejudice.

Seeing the issue of racial prejudice through a child's eyes robs it of any justification; we can only see how absurd (and harmful) it is. While adults develop an appreciation of the concept of "fairness"- which introduces the dimension of ethics into behaviour- young children do not make ethical judgments; they simply imitate their elders, or look with a completely fresh and unconditioned perspective. One advantage to Harper Lee of having Scout as so young a child is that we will not accuse Scout of being wrong, or naïve; a six-year-old does not ask whether something is right or wrong, but sees it as it is.

Scout's tendency to fight (on Christmas Day, in the playground, and, occasionally, with Jem at home) derives from a young and simple drive to stand up for her family- even without knowing what the issue is. Atticus wants her to stop using physical violence to resolve differences- because prejudice cannot be beaten out of anyone, and because, whilst some things are worth fighting over, others are not.

Scout is unable to defend herself against the majority of the aggression directed at her; the ham costume makes her vulnerable, and Mrs Dubose's insults, and those of the people in the town, cannot be stopped, as the trial comes near. In a novel about oppression, it is useful to have a six-year-old narrator to oppress!

Scout's relationships with Miss Maudie and Aunt Alexandra are rather different. Scout resists Alexandra's assumptions about white supremacy, her snobbery, and her hostility towards Calpurnia and towards any form of integration. She embraces the tolerance and liberalism of Miss Maudie. Scout the character therefore reflects the values and attitudes of Harper Lee the author; whether any real six-year-old is as enlightened as this is arguable.

As readers, we may feel that the criticism of the educational techniques and values in the school system is overdone; the use of flashcards, and the very slow adoption by pupils of reading and writing, seems only loosely connected to the plot. Miss Gates is used as a symbol of hypocrisy; she is the teacher who believes that America is a democracy in which no group or minority is mistreated.

Perhaps Harper Lee intends us to see that the lack of education- in the sense both of what is missing, and the little that is there- contributes to the passive and stupid attitudes of most of the people of Maycomb. A country which disapproves of independent reading is likely to disapprove of independent thinking; Atticus did not go to school.

Because Scout is four years younger than Jem, she is more inclined to accept what he tells her, and to be compliant. Scout overhears conversations in which her father praises her (to Uncle Jack) and defends her (to Alexandra). We admire the way in which she adheres to Atticus' demands and requests, even when the wider world is not sympathetic.

The novel, through Atticus, associates the potential for change with the children's generation- accurately, in that the civil rights protests from 1956 onwards will coincide with Scout and Jem being just either side of 30. Harper Lee skilfully attaches the emerging interest in justice (and outrage at injustice) to Jem, not Scout. However, it is not a complete success. In the rather heavy-handed discussion of the jury system in Chapter 23, the dialogue between Atticus and Jem, and in particular the questions Jem poses, are out of character. The legal argument requires an intellect much older than Jem's.

Jem's rather wide-eyed assumption that the trial will be judged on the merits of the case, and Scout's less than complete understanding of what is being said, are more convincing, in the trial chapters. Just as we can understand how oppressed and exploited the black community is, through the action of the trial and the hypocritical speeches of Alexandra, the ladies of the missionary society, and Miss Gates, so our judgment that injustice is endemic comes not from what Jem and Scout say about the trial, but from what they see and hear. If they argued about the principles more- if they were older and more articulate- there would be less drama and we would be less outraged.

The minor skirmishes Scout takes part in are to do with defending her family's honour; they are different in kind from Bob Ewell's murderous violence, or the menace of the lynch mob, which Scout defuses with her childish amiability. That episode shows that adults can be shamed out of unthinking violence when they are confronted by more enlightened, and unprejudiced, behaviour.

The innocence of childhood helps Harper Lee to challenge the (non-existent) justification for prejudice and segregation effectively in the narrative. She also needs her child characters to be capable of a more grown-up and proactive desire to change what is wrong. Jem steps out of character, into an adult voice, in Chapter 23. But, in general, putting two young children at the heart of her narrative technique enables Harper Lee to make the novel dramatic, so that it engages our emotions and sense of injustice more directly than it would if all the main characters were adults.

Some key themes and ideas in the novel

There follows now a series of themes which help us to see the values and meaning of the novel. This list is not definitive. Try rereading the novel, and making your own list, on themes which you detect.

Theme: Live and let live

...it's all about tolerating difference

Because he knows Maycomb and its people so well, **Atticus is realistic** about their attitudes and prejudices. He never "thunders" in court, and his patience and politeness disarms all except the worst of people (the Ewells).

His philosophy first emerges in Chapter 3; he tells Scout that one secret of getting on with people is to consider their perspective, "climb into (their) skin and walk around in it". Scout realises, straightaway, that **a difficulty caused by ignorance** (her teacher's, in trying to ban Scout from reading at home) **can be worked around through adopting a compromise**.

On a metaphorical level, when we read the novel, we have to climb into Scout's skin, and walk around Maycomb, so that we see it largely through the eyes of a child at primary school (although Scout is supposedly writing the book some years later, which is the 'excuse' for having more complex thoughts and sentence structures than a young child would be able to express).

Atticus tells his children that the Radleys have every right to isolate themselves. He refuses to rise to the bait of Mrs Dubose's insults or Bob Ewell's spitting on him. Just as he refuses to conform to the norms of prejudice, he gives other people the latitude to think or behave in offensive ways. This is because he understands **the effects of a lack of education, or a lack of intelligence**- which he refers to in his address to the jury in Chapter 20. He always makes allowance for other people's prejudices- except for **the two sins, of killing mockingbirds (Chapter10) and of "cheatin' a coloured man" (Chapters 20 and 23). In this book, there is very little difference between those two things, because neither the bird nor the black man (Tom) has done, or is capable of doing, any harm.**

Bob Ewell's motto, of course, is the opposite. Just as Hitler wants to persecute the Jews to extinction (chapter 26), Ewell wants the county to evict the African American population (chapter 17).

Theme: Segregation

...laws that separate, and dictate how people live, according to race

Segregation on racial grounds is depicted accurately throughout the novel. There are no black children at Scout's school. The churches, the graveyards and the seating in court are segregated. The African American community lives at "the Quarters" (near the tip) in a segregated community.

In Chapter 1, when Boo was detained after allegedly stabbing his father, the sheriff "hadn't the heart to put him in jail alongside Negroes"- in the days before prison cells were segregated, a method of informal segregation still applied.

In Chapter 3, it is clear that it is **the Ewell family who should be segregated from the rest of society, because their dirtiness and aggression really is sub-human**. No-one expects them to attend school after the first day in September. Atticus tells Scout that what we may call their self-chosen segregation does no harm, because if they want an education they can still go to school, but "it's silly to force (them) into a new environment". The problem in society is not the voluntary segregation chosen for themselves by the Ewells and the Radleys, but racial segregation, imposed by force and by prohibition.

At the end of Chapter 23, Scout and Jem discuss the unfamiliar concept of an unsegregated world. Jem's theory- that there are four types of people, or tribal groups, in the county, including the Ewells and the Cunninghams- falls apart under Scout's assertion that **differences arise only because of circumstances and opportunity, not because of inherent superiority or inferiority**. Mrs Dubose, as we see, is both an embittered racist <u>and</u> brave.

The novel's thesis- quite reasonably- is that **segregation will only be consigned to history when the adult world** sets aside its prejudices and **sees the world from a child-like perspective**. That is why the narrator of the novel is a child, or at least an adult in the persona of a child.

Theme: humour

...laughing with (and at) the characters

Scout's first teacher, Miss Caroline Fisher, disapproves of children being able to read before they come to school; being taught at home will "interfere with her reading". Her **uncomfortable lack of understanding**, of local people and their lives, **is amusing** in a slightly painful way. Her attempts to keep order and discipline Scout at the end of Chapter 2 lead to "a storm of laughter". Her terrified over-reaction to seeing a head-louse (in Chapter 3) makes her more ridiculous; as does her assumption that Burris Ewell will wash his hair properly at home, and that head-lice can be avoided in a class like this. She "mystifies" the class with stories about cats and frogs- because she does not realise that these children are "immune to imaginative literature" (Chapter 2).

Scout is so disillusioned with school that she thinks of running away from home, and she starts a long campaign to persuade Atticus to stop sending her (Chapters 3, 9).

It is **amusing** that Atticus- who is more or less unafraid of anyone- should swear Scout to secrecy over their agreement to continue to read at home; the pact is designed to keep Scout out of trouble, not him, but the narrative comes to us with a **child's perspective**.

The mythology of the Radleys' evil ability to make anything on their property fatally poisonous means that Scout licks the chewing gum in Chapter 4, and waits to die! The idea, in Chapter 4, that the children's play, "One Man's Family", runs to "Book 2, Chapter 25" is amusing; as is the way Atticus catches them trying to deliver Boo's letter on a fishing pole in Chapter 5.

At the start of Chapter 13, **Aunt Alexandra** arrives in Maycomb. This is the woman whom Scout describes in Chapter 9 as being like Mount Everest- "**cold and there**"; unemotional, looming large, quietly hostile. Now, when Jem takes **her heavy case** upstairs, it **hits the floor "with a thump" which has "a dull permanence"- she is immovable.**

Her subsequent attempts to train Scout in **lady-like behaviour**, and to make Atticus' children conscious of their position in Maycomb society, are **grimly humorous**, and doomed to fail, because Atticus is democratic, and she is merely autocratic. Alexandra thinks that she is needed, to provide "some feminine influence"; she underestimates the role of Calpurnia, whom she wants Atticus to sack (Chapter 14). She disapproves of Atticus' liberal attitudes, as a parent, and she wants to insulate his children from the wider world. She wants to make them feel superior, because of their family history, but Atticus undermines this, with his **subversive tale of the mentally ill cousin Joshua**, and he tells his children to "forget" whatever she has to tell them of their family history. For Atticus, no-one has a valid claim to be regarded as superior to others, and we are wrong to regard ourselves as superior. **It is absurd that Bob Ewell regards himself and his family as superior to anybody.**

In all of these instances, **Harper Lee attaches humour to what she thinks is dysfunctional.**

Note that Atticus is nowhere and never a figure of fun or the butt of jokes. There is nothing ridiculous about him because there is nothing 'wrong' with how he lives his life.

Theme: education

...what is and is not learnt at school in Maycomb (and what needs to be!)

In Maycomb, children start at school at the age of six (Chapter 1).

After primary school, there is a state industrial school, which provides the best secondary education. There is an engineering school at Auburn. Children have to pass a class before going up to the next grade. Walter Cunningham has not been able to go up from the first grade because he has been needed to help his father on their farm, but now a younger child can take on what he has been doing.

Scout starts school in Chapter 2. Her teacher is hopelessly naïve, and has to impose a new, **ineffective** reading scheme which makes reading at home "illicit"! Scout feels that being able to read is a "crime". Miss Fisher says that whatever Atticus has taught her is "damage", because he "does not know how to teach" (and she does?).

Children do not write until they are aged eight- they print instead. The Dewey system of teaching that is used here is lampooned, again, at the start of Chapter 4; it promises Scout twelve years of tedium, because it achieves so little so slowly.

While Miss Fisher is ineffectual because she is so young, **Miss Gates** (Chapter 26) is a hypocrite who sees America as democratic and Hitler as an extremist. She **does not stop to** think that oppressing the Jews is essentially identical to oppressing the African Americans.

The consistent criticism of school education (which Atticus avoided) has a deeper meaning; **it is no wonder that racism exists when it is educated into children, by not tackling the hypocrisy of American domestic and community values.**

Theme: Ancestry and origins

...making the case against racism!

Southerners like to be able to trace their ancestors back through many generations, and ideally to 1066 (Chapter 1), which, of course, is impossible. Ancestry or "background", for Aunt Alexandra, gives you status in society.

Miss Maudie Atkinson says (Chapter 24) that "background"- or **value in society- does not depend on family history, but on the values of fairness and humility**. Without those values, you are worthless, as the Ewells certainly are, according to Heck Tate, in Chapter 29- and to us as readers throughout the novel.

Atticus's sister Alexandra is as much of a racist and a snob as Bob Ewell, but a little less obviously so. The disease of racism means that, as Maudie says, there is only a small number of people in Maycomb who have real "background" or the courage to fight against it- most notably, Atticus.

Simon Finch, Atticus's ancestor, owned three slaves. But Atticus regards Cal as his children's surrogate mother- they are to obey her just as much as they are to obey him or his sister.

Atticus, and his brother Jack, take a Darwinian view of human history. They think that all races originated from Africa, or Egypt; that all races were black originally; and that the false sense of history and culture which the southern states perpetuate is absolutely worthless (Chapter 13).

Atticus and his sister agree that **the Ewells are "trash". For her, it's because they have no "gentle breeding"; for him, it is because they treat other people so badly.** The novel tells us that Alexandra, with her preoccupation with heredity, tradition and breeding, is wrong. Whoever you are, "breeding" is about behaving as a gentleman, as Jem would say; being brave and fair, as Atticus would say; being trusted in your community, as Miss Maudie would say; or being like Tom Robinson. Good breeding is simply being humble and respectable.

Theme: social attitudes

...generally accepted beliefs that shape our characters' everyday behaviour

In Chapter 3, Scout is critical of Walter Cunningham's table manners (he pours syrup over all his food). When Calpurnia tells her that she must not criticise a guest, she says "He's just a Cunningham"; his lower social status means that the normal rules of politeness do not apply to him. (She is not however, allowed to get away with this belief, by her father or Cal). Compare this with Atticus' account of Tom Robinson's shooting, in Chapter 24; escaping prisoners can be shot seventeen times (because it doesn't matter; why not?).

Atticus is blind to issues of colour. Calpurnia may be employed as a cook, but she is indispensable to his family for more than household tasks- he tells Scout (in Chapter 3) and Alexandra (in

Chapter 14) that they will never dispense with her. She is, essentially, a member of the family. This contrasts with Mrs Merriweather's patronising attitude to her cook, Sophy, in Chapter 24; she thinks that employing her for a dollar and a quarter a week is an act of charity.

The contempt and distaste in the white community for "nigger-loving" or "lawing for niggers" is shared by Maycomb's people of all ages and classes- Mrs Dubose, Aunt Alexandra, Cecil Jacobs, Bob Ewell, Francis Hancock. Only Miss Maudie stands apart from this prejudice.

The missionary society ladies, in Chapter 24, betray their own hypocrisy. They are quite unaware of their own prejudices and intolerance. Jem suggests (end of Chapter 23) that **Boo Radley may not want to come out, because the prejudices of the community alienate him**. Although the Radleys and Atticus are different in other ways, **Boo and Atticus are both good neighbours, responsible citizens, and people who do not allow the prevailing disease of Maycomb- its prejudice- infect them.**

Theme: Prohibition

...law that forbids alcohol

There was a ban, from 1920 to 1933, on producing, selling or transporting alcohol in the USA. It was supported by Methodists and Baptists, and by the Ku Klux Klan. It is just ending as this book begins. Miss Maudie, however, puts alcohol in her cakes, and Dill's aunt Rachel appears to drink large amounts of whisky in the mornings. Atticus is a non-drinker. The supply of alcohol was legalised again by President Roosevelt in March 1933, partly as a measure to help stimulate the official (as opposed to the black market) economy. In F Scott Fitzgerald's novel, "The Great Gatsby", Jay Gatsby's wealth is alleged to have been generated by the illegal sale or bootlegging of alcohol.

Theme: Fights and shooting

…how aggression motivates some characters

Burris Ewell's aggression towards his teacher in Chapter 3 anticipates Bob Ewell's aggression towards Atticus, Judge Taylor and Helen Robinson. Little Chuck has no interest in negotiating with any Ewell, and would be happy to kill Burris. Heck Tate expresses exactly the same opinion about Bob Ewell in Chapter 29, where he calls him a "low-down skunk". Ironically, in trying to kill Atticus' children, Ewell leaves his own orphaned (and better off!).

While Nathan Radley fires his shotgun, to protect his property from intruders, and Atticus shoots the dog Tim Johnson to protect the community from rabies, **Atticus** himself **believes that to have a gun is to invite someone to shoot you.**

Atticus' response to crises is to be polite, mild and non-confrontational. He wants Scout to grow out of physical fights. He will not teach his own children how to shoot, although he is especially well qualified to do that. He would like them to shoot at tin cans, but he recognises the attraction of moving targets. Bluejays can be shot; mockingbirds cannot.

Tom Robinson is shot (seventeen times) in an act of needless aggression; he could have been rearrested outside the prison. Atticus knows that Jem could have been shot when he went back to fetch his trousers from the Radleys' (Chapter 26). Scout and Jem are frustrated that their father does not shoot, and they are impressed when they see that he can, and how skilful he is at it (Chapter 10).

Atticus rejects violence as an unjustified means by which the strong oppress the defenceless. No-one apart from Tom Robinson is shot (despite the strange tale of the suicide by shotgun of Dolphus Raymond's bride in Chapter 16).

Consider this in the light of the publication of the novel in 1960, and the emergence of Martin Luther King as a civil rights campaign leader in the 1956 Montgomery Bus Boycott. **Atticus' dogma of securing change by non-violent means makes him Maycomb's (white) Martin Luther King.**

Theme: Ghosts

...using a child's natural imagination to good effect.

Boo Radley is described as a "malevolent phantom" in Chapter 1 (but not in Chapter 28, where Bob Ewell is the invisible, evil stalker, and Boo is the children's saviour). A myth, made up by Dill, surrounds him; that he is some species of animal-eating Frankenstein's monster who only comes out at night, looks like a skull, and that he is kept chained to the bed most of the time. Dill builds on this to characterise him as even more grotesque.

Only a child's imagination can do this. When Scout finally sees Boo, at the end of Chapter 29, she knows who he is. He does not need to identify himself.

Atticus says that "there were other ways of making people into ghosts". Both Tom Robinson and his widow Helen are made into ghosts, through the oppression of the Ewells and the jury. They become the living dead, because they are in despair and without hope; then Tom is shot.

Despite the talk about haints (a colloquial term for haunts or ghosts) and hot steams- in connection with walking past the Radleys'- and Aunt Alexandra's premonition that the night of the pageant will end badly, there is very little of the supernatural in the novel. Despite the religiosity of Maycomb, the culture is that when you're dead, you're dead; anything else is superstition.

Bob Ewell's threats of revenge are as haunting as a ghost, from Chapter 23 onwards.

Theme: Superstitions

...behaviours that people adopt to deal with things that they can't readily explain

The idea that the Radleys' house is an evil place means that black people will cross the road and whistle, instead of walking past it at night (out of fear of evil spirits). The Radleys' trees are thought to yield poisonous pecan nuts. Jem says that Boo is a haint (Chapter 3).

Jem believes that Indian-head pennies bring good luck because they have magical properties. He also believes in Hot Steams-spots in hot, isolated places at night, where ghosts in purgatory (the space between earth and heaven, or earth and hell) loiter, and where you must recite an injunction for them not to suck your breath. Scout tells Dill that Calpurnia describes that superstition as "nigger-talk".

The novel shows us that the racism which condemns Tom is just as irrational as any superstition. The legal prohibition of mixed race marriage and the widespread fear, among white women, of rape- which was at the heart of the Scottsboro trials, and which Harper Lee turns on its head, through the behaviour of Mayella, to make it even more groundless- has no justification. Atticus' closing speech in Chapter 20 is important. It is the uneducated, mean-spirited and prejudiced who maintain that "*all* Negroes are basically immoral beings, that *all* Negro men are not to be trusted around our women".

The complicated architecture of racism and segregation is built out of nothing except superstition.

Theme: Families

… how the characters group together in their homes

Atticus is a single parent; Calpurnia, Miss Maudie and his sister are each, in some way, surrogate mothers for his children. Atticus' brother, Uncle Jack, has never been married and has no desire to.

Dill has a mother and stepfather who do not care much for him, and an alcoholic aunt.

Miss Fisher and Miss Gates are responsible for the education of Maycomb's white children, but they have no children of their own.

Judge Taylor is married, but he and his wife don't kiss much. Miss Maudie (despite confusingly being called Miss) is a widow. Stephanie Crawford has a wooden, wood-carving male friend (in the country). There is no Mrs Bob Ewell, just as there is no Mrs Atticus Finch.

Since old Mrs Radley died, Nathan and Boo Radley have lived by themselves. Perhaps Alexandra should have tried to impose her feminine influence on them, instead of on her brother's household!

Calpurnia has grown up children, but there is no mention of her husband.

In my view, **it is no accident that none of these families is complete**. Their incompleteness confirms and underpins the lack of warmth, humanity and love in the lives of most of Maycomb's residents. Hardness breeds more hardness of spirit.

The only fully functional family unit in the novel is that of Tom and Helen Robinson, and their three children- until that, too, is disfigured by Tom's killing.

The themes and ideas you've just read about all help to bind the narrative together, and they enable us to think a little like a resident of Maycomb.

Next, we need to note how Harper Lee uses characterisation. Put this book down for a few minutes, and make your own list of the characters who are good and the ones who are bad. Do you expect there to be a majority of "bad" characters, or "good" ones? Do you agree with my view that Maycomb itself is a bad place?

Here are my lists; it may surprise you to discover that they come out remarkably evenly balanced in terms of the numbers.

Good characters- Atticus, Scout, Jem, Cal, Uncle Jack, Miss Maudie, Boo Radley, Tom Robinson, Helen Robinson, Judge Taylor, Rev Sykes, Heck Tate, Dolphus Raymond, Link Deas, Mr Underwood, Walter Cunningham Snr, Walter Cunningham Jnr. Total- 18

Bad characters- Bob Ewell, Mayella Ewell, Burris Ewell, Aunt Alexandra, Uncle Jimmy, Francis Hancock, Cecil Jacobs, Stephanie Crawford, Rachel Haverford, Nathan Radley, Mr Gilmer, Lula, Mrs Dubose, Mr Avery, Miss Caroline Fisher, Miss Gates, Mrs Farrow, Mrs Merriweather. Total- 18

And the moral is, as Atticus would tell us, that bad people and good people can and do live side by side.

The character names (of the good and the not so good)

...and their origins in the author's life and times

Harper Lee's mother was called Frances Cunningham Finch. This explains why the Cunninghams are relatively decent people, and why Scout is a Finch.

Her father, AC Lee, had been a newspaper editor and owner before he became a lawyer; perhaps this explains Atticus' extreme fondness for the local papers!

Mr Lee went on to be a lawyer who served in the Alabama State Legislature from 1926 to 1938 (just like Atticus); and, early in his career, he defended, unsuccessfully, two black men accused of murdering a white storekeeper.

This may have influenced the idea for the trial of Tom Robinson, as well as the reference, in chapter one, to the execution of Atticus' first two clients (Haverfords), on a murder charge.

All about Maycomb

This sleepy small town in the deep South is old, tired, and sweltering in the heat- apart from the first snow since 1885, which falls in Chapter 8. People move slowly. A day seems longer than 24 hours; "there was nowhere to go, nothing to buy and no money to buy it with". The town has no cinema, although it shows religious films in the court-house now and again. The Finch household has a radio; there is no television. Court cases and trials are a form of public entertainment. There is very little going on.

Chapter 13 explains that it is an ancient town, designed as a local government centre, so it is a natural home for the professions- lawyers, dentists, mechanics, doctors, bankers, counsellors, vets. But it is off the beaten track, and so it has remained the same size for a hundred years. When it grew, "it grew inward"; no new blood meant intermarriage. Family attitudes and behaviours are fossilised, giving rise to proverb-type sayings about clans and families - there is a "caste system" among the white families; another form of segregation, but based on social superiority, not alleged racial superiority.

Atticus' wife, a Graham from Montgomery, falls into the category of outsiders. The occasional arrival of such people is not enough to disturb "the quiet stream of family resemblance"- the pattern of everything staying the same.

Chapter 28 contains an account of (the fictional) Colonel Maycomb, after whom the (fictional) town took its name. He is not heroic, but over-confident and incompetent; he mistook north-west for south in a military campaign. Is it an accident that this town, with its sense of confusion, and all of its lack of a sense of human geography, is named after him?

The Characters

The Three Main Children

Scout (Jean Louise Finch)

Because she is the narrator of the novel, Scout's character is not deepened by what other people say about her when she is not present.

Her tomboy tendencies serve to put the notion of fragrant, elegant but heartless "Southern womanhood" under the microscope. Scout is reluctant to conform to Alexandra's forced formality ("the starched walls of a pink cotton penitentiary"- Chapter 14).

She is a breaker of rules (swearing and fist-fights), and- more importantly- a breaker down of barriers. She challenges Alexandra's assumptions that Walter Cunningham is an inappropriate friend, and that visiting Calpurnia's home is undesirable. Scout promotes social mobility and equality; she has learned this from Atticus. It makes the crucial difference, when she manages to defuse the ugly scene outside the jail in Chapter 15.

Despite her interest in becoming a cheerleader in the High School marching band (Chapter 11), Scout's focus is on reading, and on her own family. She readily absorbs information from Miss Maudie. At school, she helps Miss Caroline Fisher to understand the context of rural life in poverty-struck Maycomb; and she helps Walter Cunningham Senior to see that he has a long-standing and respectful relationship with Atticus, which invalidates his instinct to lynch Tom.

At moments of stress or distress, Scout seeks Atticus out for comfort and reassurance. She stands up for herself when Uncle Jack accuses her, wrongly, of picking a fight with Francis Hancock (Chapter 9). This fearlessness- in refusing to submit to unreasonable demands, and challenging misconceptions and unfairness- will stand her in good stead, as she grows up into Maycomb's next Miss Maudie.

Dill

His real name is Charles Baker Harris.

He can read. He is aged almost seven in Chapter 1. He looks "right puny" (Jem).

He comes from Meridian, Mississippi. He spends the summer of 1933 with his aunt Rachel, and will do so in future years. His family were from Maycomb County originally. His mother worked for a photographer in Meridian. He has seen the film of Dracula; perhaps this is where his gothic imaginings about Boo Radley and his diet of cats and squirrels come from.

He wears blue linen shorts. His hair is snow white, and stuck to his head, like duck-fluff; he has blue eyes.

He says he hasn't got a father, but his father isn't dead (unexplained, in Chapter 1). He has "eccentric plans, strange longings, and quaint fancies". He tells enormous lies, according to Scout.

Francis Hancock tells Scout that Dill has no home of his own, and is simply passed from one to another of his relatives.

In Chapter 12, Dill sends Scout a letter saying he has a new father, a lawyer, much younger than Atticus. In Chapter 14, he has his own "twilight world" of the imagination.

Dill invents the schemes to make Boo come out of his house. He is a creative liar (Jem's trousers) and an inventor of fiction. Perhaps it is no accident that he is modelled on Harper Lee's childhood friend, the writer Truman Capote.

Jem (Jeremy Atticus Finch)

We are aware of his broken arm at the start of the novel. He thinks Boo Radley looks like Frankenstein .

He never declines a dare.

Of his growing up process, he says it is like being "a caterpillar in a cocoon" (Chapter 22). Chapter 11 describes him as having "a naturally tranquil disposition and a slow fuse".

Note the resemblance between his arm injury and Tom Robinson's (Chapter 18).

Jem loses his faith in the adult world, in Chapters 22-23. He has started to question some of Atticus' instructions- to go home when the lynch mob assembles, for example- and he is (rightly) worried about Bob Ewell's threats of revenge.

He aspires to be a lawyer and to be like his father, apart from Atticus' lack of athleticism. He develops a teenage obsession with sport. By turns, he is frustrated with Scout and protective of her. We see the assumptions of Jem's childhood- that Maycomb is a safe and well-intentioned place- tested and corrected, through his experience of the injustice of Mrs Dubose and then the trial.

Ewell's vengeance leaves its mark, not on Atticus, but on Jem. His broken arm will always be a reminder of the wrongs done to Tom Robinson.

Atticus Finch

Atticus has a "profound distaste for the practice of criminal law". He tells his children that they are both right about the events leading to Jem's broken arm. He grew up at Finch's Landing with his older sister Alexandra and his younger brother Jack. He went to Montgomery to study law, and became a barrister.

Once established as a lawyer, he has made a reasonable income in Maycomb, because his roots were there and he was always well known and trusted; more than that, he "was related by blood or marriage to nearly every family in the town". This helps to explain why he considers them generally good people.

The Finches live on the main residential street. His children find him "satisfactory"- he plays with them, reads to them, "and treated us with courteous detachment".

His wife died when Scout was two; she was a Graham from Montgomery. Atticus met her when he was first elected to the state legislature. He was middle-aged then, and she was 15 years younger than him. Jem was born in the first year of their marriage, Scout was six when she died of a heart attack- a health defect which was said to run in her family.

Atticus tells Jem that you don't need to tie Boo to a bed- there are "other ways of making people into ghosts"; he means by denying them their right to be treated fairly and without prejudice.

He uses "amiable silence" to prise from Scout what is worrying her. Jem cannot keep from him the real nature of the games to make Boo come out (Chapter 5), just as Bob and Mayella Ewell cannot keep the truth hidden, under his cross-examination. Atticus is wise, and not easily fooled.

He is aged almost 50 at the start of Chapter 10; much older than the parents of the other children at school, and the fact that he works in an office does not inspire the admiration of his own children.

He wears glasses, and his sight in his left eye is impaired- a genetic family characteristic. His sole recreation is reading, not the hunting, fishing, betting at cards, smoking or drinking which tends to occupy the other men of the town.

He is a public figure because of his second job in the state legislature. Because of this role, he commands widespread respect, and he also judges himself by his own, uniquely high, standards of personal morality.

Atticus is a traditionalist in many ways. He is content with the rape laws, and he has an old-fashioned, classical Southern gentility. But he is a modernist in some important ways.

He believes that people are fundamentally unequal in intelligence and ability- and that this principle cannot nor particularly should be challenged. See what he says about the education system in Chapter 20. This means that, for Atticus, notions of white supremacy need to be overcome- there is nothing inherently superior about white people. He points out that racism is wrong, because we all belong to one race- the human race.

Exploiting people makes you "trash"; white people should never use racist power in the way Bob Ewell does. Atticus treats Calpurnia and the Robinsons with the same respect he would anyone else. This principle of treating everyone as equal extends to the way he treats his children; it is the opposite of Maycomb's traditional ways of doing things.

While Atticus is a rule-maker, he is also a trail-blazer in his remorseless opposition to unfairness and injustice. He understands that, because people are flawed and prejudiced, there will be evil outcomes from time to time; the answer is to follow your conscience, which he always does, but too few of his fellow-citizens have, so far, learned to do.

The Ewells – Bob and his children, Burris and Mayella

This family is first mentioned in chapter 1- Scout says that she still believes that the Ewells started the episode which led to Jem's broken arm. The first of them we encounter is Burris Ewell (Chapter 3) - the filthiest human Scout had ever seen. Other children say that he has no mother and that his father is "right contentious" (argumentative).

Burris is "hard-down mean"- aggressively unpleasant. Atticus explains to Scout that evening that three generations of the Ewells have been the disgrace of Maycomb, never working, and living "like animals". The law does not apply to them, because they are "an exclusive society made up of Ewells". They refuse to be bound by any reasonable code of behaviour.

They do not have to go to school, like everyone else, and Bob Ewell is permitted to hunt and trap out of season, because otherwise his children would starve, as Mr Ewell spends his benefits on whisky.

Is it because the law is bent, to allow him to hunt out of season (illegally), so that his children do not starve, that he thinks he can lie in court (which is also illegal, and an offence called perjury), in order to have Tom Robinson convicted of a non-existent crime?

Chapter 13 informs us that the Ewells have lived on the same plot of land behind the tip, on welfare, for three generations. They live in a shack which was once "a Negro cabin". It is made of wood and corrugated iron, and it is propped up on four stone blocks. It has no proper windows, and just a small hall and four tiny rooms. The fence is made from wooden items from the tip, and amidst the assorted rubbish in the garden is a wreck of a car, without wheels.

The only redeeming feature- the only human touch- is a set of six chipped jars, containing brilliant red geraniums, which Mayella Ewell looks after. She is a gardener, rather like Miss Maudie Atkinson.

The number of Ewell children is estimated, variously, as six or nine. Mayella says there are eight, including her, of whom two can read and write.

Bob Ewell's full name is "Robert E Lee Ewell"- he is named after the general who led the pro-slavery Confederate Army in the American Civil War. Atticus has already said, half-humorously, that people named after Confederate generals become "slow, steady drinkers". Ewell attacks the children when made bold by whisky.

He is a "little bantam cock of a man", "a red little rooster" with a red neck (redneck is a name for a person with no intelligence). He has little hair, a thin, pointed nose, and a wrinkled neck with no real chin. The authorial voice in Chapter 17 informs us that there is a family like the Ewells in every small town. They never work or go to school; they are never free of illnesses caused by their "filthy surroundings". They have "congenital defects". They are scum, or white trash.

Mayella Violet Ewell is aged 19, "a thick-bodied girl accustomed to strenuous labour". Unlike her father, she looks as though she tries to keep clean.

The Cunninghams from Old Sarum

An enormous and confusing tribe domiciled in the north part of the country. The wrong crowd. To begin with, there were two families-the Cunninghams and the Coninghams- who intermarried, and became indistinguishable, because they could not spell well enough to keep their identities separate.

Walter Cunningham is in Scout's class; on the first day of school, she has to explain to their teacher why he has no lunch (he has a skinny jaw because he is undernourished, and he will not accept her telling him to borrow money from her). He has no shoes and has hookworms. His father leads the lynch mob which Atticus resists in Chapter 15. Atticus says that Cunningham Snr (a client of his, who has no money) has "blind spots"- racism and mob violence. Alexandra labels the Cunninghams as "drunk and disorderly".

The Cunninghams are better people than the Ewells because, although neither family has shoes, a Cunningham child goes to school on the first day of the school year in clean, mended clothes (Chapter 2). Unlike the Ewells, who will take anything they can get their hands on, the Cunninghams always repay their debts, and manage on what little they have.

Walter Cunningham Snr leads the ominous lynch mob in Chapter 15. He is ready to harm Atticus in order to murder Tom Robinson before his trial can take place. He cannot go through with this plan, however, because Scout's interest in him, and her helpful approach to his son's lack of a school lunch, gives her the power to defuse the confrontation.

The Cunninghams are decent people, who get by on the little they have, honour their debts, and finally (improbably) seek to acquit Tom on the rape charge. Atticus regards them as "our friends", but he knows they are also susceptible to mad and prejudiced behaviour in any context where racism can find a voice.

The Radleys – Boo and Nathan

Brothers Boo and Nathan Radley have no interest in social contact, and no interest in their house maintenance. The overall effect, of tatty neglect, is to leave their house "droopy and sick".

Boo seems to the children to be a malevolent phantom. He is never seen. People have said that he was evil or cursed; so much so that superstitions are held by white people against him.

This is not a new set of habits; even many years before, the Radleys were very private, and they did not go to church, or make social visits.

Old Mr Radley would walk to the town at 11.30 and return at 12 with groceries. They had always lived in that particular house, with their two sons. Then the older one, Nathan, lived in Pensacola, and visited his parents at Christmas.

As a teenager, the younger boy fell in with a gang of Cunninghams from Old Sarum; they were all arrested for disorderly conduct; and all sent to the state industrial school (where a good education was available to them). The school was not a prison, and no disgrace attached to being sent there, but Mr Radley guaranteed that, if the judge released him, Arthur would give no more trouble to anybody. His father then kept him inside the house for 15 years. A thin leathery man with colourless eyes, sharp cheekbones, a wide mouth, and an upright walk, Mr Radley never spoke to the children, but just coughed to acknowledge them. His death is related in Chapter 1; Cal calls him "the meanest man".

Miss Maudie Atkinson gives Scout the Radleys' history in Chapter 5- they are strict Baptists, and, because of their ideological/religious objection to the idea of fun or pleasure, their house is "sad".

Boo Radley may (or may not) have been mentally ill when, at the age of 33 he stabbed his father in the leg with a pair of scissors. Boo is probably around 40 at the time the novel begins. By this time, he is mentally challenged: he views the world as a child and tries to "play" with the three real children by leaving gifts and interesting objects in the hollow of a tree.

When we finally do see Boo Radley – after he saves the children from Bob Ewell – he is pale but normal-looking. However, Scout recounts that she never sees him again – so we presume that he simply returns to his (self-imposed?) exile inside the Radley's House.

Boo's character functions on two main levels: first, it drives the plot (it allows us to see the range of a child's imagination; and it means the children are saved from the evil, murderous intentions of Bob Ewell); secondly, it shows that people can be hounded and badly treated due to mental illness as well as racism- neither prejudice is justified. Boo shows himself to be brave and upright when he saves the children from danger – yet the popular gossip would have had us believe that he was, himself, a dangerous menace!

Miss Maudie Atkinson

An important character; an ally of Atticus, she is relaxed about the way he brings his children up. She is friendly to Scout and Jem, and a source of information and support for them. She is never intimidated, always liberal in her attitudes, and quite direct in criticising silliness.

She lets the children play in her garden and keeps a cow. She is a widow who spends the days gardening in an old straw hat and men's coveralls, then sits in the evening "in magisterial beauty". She wages a ruthless war on nutgrass. She has gold prongs clipped to her eye-teeth. She makes the best cakes in the neighbourhood (they are laced with alcohol). She grew up with Uncle Jack at Finch's Landing (and so is about ten years younger than Atticus). Her father was a landowner and doctor. She has "an acid tongue", but she tells no tales. She is always friendly, but her voice "was enough to shut anybody up".

She is remarkably positive when her house burns down (Atticus has said that she has almost nothing else i.e. no money); she tells Jem it gives her more garden, and she will be able to have a smaller house, and finance it with two lodgers. She will stay with Miss Stephanie Crawford for the time being, but will continue to keep her cake recipes secret.

She refuses to go to watch Tom Robinson's trial, because she considers it a "morbid" spectacle, "like a Roman carnival"- in other words, like watching a gladiator or a Christian being fed to the lions in a one-sided, fatal piece of entertainment. She knows that there is no chance that Atticus will win the case.

It is through what Miss Maudie says about him that Harper Lee shapes our appreciation of Atticus' character and his moral principles.

Miss Stephanie Crawford

The source of most of Jem's information about Boo Radley; a neighbourhood scold. She encourages the myth that Boo creeps out at night.

She goes about doing good, but no one trusts her. She is "old"; she has a sweetheart who carves with wood and lives down the country. She is fat in the middle, with little-bitty arms.

She cannot resist going to watch the trial, dressed up in a hat and gloves, to see what Atticus is up to. She takes exception to the fact that the children were there at all, and sitting in the coloured balcony, breaking the convention of segregation. She thinks Atticus may have sent them to sit there as a statement- which is another of her conspiracy theories.

Her tendency to gossip is as wide as the English Channel (Chapter 25); there is nothing it will not swallow up.

Judge John Taylor

He appears in the trial, from Chapter 16 onwards. He looks like a sleepy old shark. He is amiable, white-haired, red-faced. He cleans his nails while evidence is being given; chews cigars;

appears to be asleep, and puts his feet up; but is "learned in the law" and therefore reliable. He is close to 70.

He is a composite character, who may reflect aspects of the behaviour of one or more of the several judges in the Scottsboro trials (Hawkins, Horton, Callahan).

Atticus says that Judge Taylor had tried to influence the jury, by making Bob Ewell look ridiculous; it is debatable whether we detect this when we read the court scenes. But Miss Maudie knows that, because he appointed Atticus to defend Tom, the judge is on the side of equality and desegregation (Chapter 22).

Heck Tate

The sheriff of Maycomb County. He is as tall as Atticus, but thinner, with a long nose. He has a heavy rifle and a belt with bullets.

He is the first witness at the trial (Chapter 16), where he wears a suit and glasses, and looks harmless. He is aged 42 at the end of novel. He is married.

He appears at moments of crisis- he relies on Atticus to shoot the dog, and he resolves the issue of justice for Boo, by overriding Atticus' sense of what is legally proper, at the end of the novel. His "unschooled and blunt" stubbornness here is necessary for the plot. Just as Atticus recognises that it is pointless applying the law to the Ewells' poaching and truancy from school, Tate knows that the law needs to be bent to protect the privacy (and sanity) of the reclusive and damaged Boo. He will not allow Boo to be turned into a mockingbird, or a helpless victim of the mob, as Tom had been.

Importantly, Harper Lee gets him out of the way for the drama in Chapter 15; Atticus has to face the lynch mob alone because they have sent Mr Tate "on a snipe hunt" (a wild goose chase).

Tom Robinson

Tom is aged 25, married with three children; a member of Calpurnia's church; he is clean-living, respectable, humble and helpful.

Rather like Boo, Tom has a mythology around him (arising from the mere accusation of rape) which simply dissolves as soon as he makes his delayed appearance on the stage of the novel.

The court gives him no credit for his decency and selflessness, because their stereotyped view of black men is so strongly embedded. Tom's good manners and integrity as a witness show that he is no criminal- quite apart from the physical disability which makes it impossible for him to have committed the alleged assault.

Tom's loss of hope, and his lapse into despair over the legal appeal (which Atticus thinks they would win), is necessary to the plot, to motivate his attempted escape and his outrageous shooting. It is interesting that Harper Lee uses that incident in two opposite ways; it motivates Braxton Underwood's morally upright indignation (Chapter 25), but it also reinforces the judgment that it is "typical of a nigger to cut and run". Even Tom's well-developed sensibilities simply serve to reinforce the unthinking racial stereotyping.

Tom puts up with the hostile and insulting questions of Horace Gilmer in Chapter 19 with the same poise and calmness Atticus shows, when Bob Ewell spits on him. Martin Luther King's method to win civil rights was to oppose oppression with non-violent resistance. Both Atticus and Tom anticipate him in this.

By the middle of October 1935, Tom Robinson has been forgotten in Maycomb (Chapter 27).

Calpurnia

She is described as all angles and bones; short-sighted, and squinting. She rarely comments on the ways of white people. Scout tells us that when she was furious her grammar became erratic; otherwise, it was as good as anybody's in Maycomb.

She is very much a surrogate mother for Scout and Jem. She is a few years (but not many) older than Atticus (Chapter 12). She grew up at Finch's Landing and moved to Maycomb with Atticus when he was married. She has been the family's cook since Jem was born; so, even before Atticus' wife died.

She features less prominently in the novel as a whole than we might think. Her main chapters are 10, where she takes the lead in resolving the danger of the rabid dog, and 12, where she takes Jem and Scout to her church.

She is utterly reliable and trustworthy; it is clear that she is genuinely fond of Atticus' children. She taught Scout to write, and is a positive influence. She organises the children's routine in a way which Atticus might not, even if he were not out working.

Atticus tells anyone who will listen that Cal is indispensable to his family; she is a servant in name only. Where there is no

143

segregation, just mutual respect, the "human race", as Atticus calls it, will be integrated, regardless of the colour of people's skin. The Finch household, with Cal in it, is a small-scale model which proves that segregation- much as Alexandra approves of it- is unnecessary and divisive.

Aunt Alexandra

She is Introduced in Chapter 9 as "uncompromising"- and described as such again at the end of Chapter 12. She is married to Uncle Jimmy, whom Scout ignores, as does she; they have an adult son, whose child Francis is.

Scout thinks she is more like a Crawford than a Finch, but she is really like Mount Everest- always "cold and there". She has the Finch family's characteristic sharp nose and chin.

She disapproves of Atticus' style of being a parent; she thinks Scout should dress femininely. She creates tension, but Atticus is unaffected by her opinions. Alexandra discriminates against Scout, because she is a girl; while she allows Jem and Francis to eat with the adults, she sends Scout to eat the Christmas meal at a separate, small table. She uses segregation in her own house, on children!

She is not fat, but solid and formidable- she is irritable on Sundays because she wears a corset.

She has boarding-school manners and is an incurable gossip. She is "one of the last of her kind" (Chapter 13). She does not know the meaning of self-doubt (meaning that she is arrogant); she never feels bored because she always has something to do- to "arrange, advise, caution, and warn".

She believes herself to be a great judge and characteriser of others; she feels that all of the old Maycomb families have their own characteristics which pass from each generation to the next- such as drinking, gambling, meanness, humour, busybodying. Scout thinks that her obsession with heredity is odd; we can see that it is a way of expressing, unconsciously, her resistance to social change.

She is treated as a figure of fun in the narrative- Atticus suggests that, by her code of definitions, the Finch family must have an incestuous streak. She does not understand the joke, because she has no sense of humour.

She turns the Finch household into a social hub for "Maycomb ladies", but she ignores the children, who see her only at mealtimes and bedtime. We should remember that her excuse for staying is to bring a feminine outlook into the house, for the benefit of the children. In that, she fails.

In Chapter 16, she says that children who go outdoors at night are a disgrace to the family, and that Mr Underwood's protection of Atticus (with his shotgun) meant that Jem and Scout had contributed nothing to resolving the conflict with the Cunningham mob. This is a preconceived judgment, and it is wrong.

She defines Walter Cunningham as "trash" in Chapter 23- incorrectly. She thinks that value derives from social status; we know, as Atticus does, that the term "trash" means the absence of moral values. Scout and Jem discuss her error towards the end of the chapter.

Throughout the novel, Alexandra's conventional, formal and unintelligent approach to life gives rise to contrasts between her and Miss Maudie, and her and Atticus. These comparisons are always to Alexandra's disadvantage.

Minor characters

Mr Dolphus Raymond

He has constructed a myth about himself, that he is permanently drunk, so that people will ignore his inter-racial relationship. We only discover this truth in Chapter 20 - it is an example (as with Mrs Dubose's unpleasantness) of hidden motivation, and of truths which are not known to Scout and Jem. Mr Raymond is not a drunk; Tom is not a rapist.

He "lurched" past the Finches' house on horseback, and Jem believes he is "drunk 'fore eight in the morning".

Chapter 16 reveals that he lives with a black woman and has mixed race children. He owns one side of the riverbank and comes from an old, wealthy Maycomb family.

A myth attaches to him, that, on discovering that he intended to keep his black mistress, his (white) bride killed herself on the day of the rehearsal of their wedding. This seems very improbable; it shows that the white community feels the need to explain away, not accept, his approach. Rather as with Boo Radley's isolation, a tall tale grows up to explain a behaviour which the community cannot come to terms with.

Tom Robinson almost died after his arm was caught in a cotton gin (a piece of machinery) owned by Dolphus.

John Hale Finch (Uncle Jack)

Atticus' brother- he is ten years younger than Atticus. Every Christmas Eve, Atticus fetches him from the station and he stays for a week. He is a doctor, with a fund of amusing stories. He is unmarried, but has a yellow cat called Rose Aylmer.

He has the same belief in fairness and moral leadership as Atticus. He tells Scout off for swearing.

His liberalism extends to an important belief which he shares with Atticus. It is mentioned in Chapter 16. He has told Jem that the Finch family's origins cannot be traced further back than any other family's, and that they may well have originated in Ethiopia in the time of the Old Testament. This doctrine of equality is put to us just before the start of the trial, to highlight how ahead of its time it is.

It is consistent with Scout's report, in Chapter 23, that Atticus told her that every family is equally old (so that notions of background or superiority have no basis).

Mr Underwood

He is the owner, editor and printer of the Maycomb Tribune. He "despises Negroes, won't have one near him", and is an intense, profane little man, with bitter eyes. As a child, Harper Lee had an

Underwood typewriter, which makes the newspaper editor's surname an apt little joke.

Near the end of Chapter 25, Mr Underwood has a surprising change of heart. He writes an editorial condemning the shooting of Tom. This is based on the behaviour of a real editor of the Montgomery Advertiser, Grover C Hall (1888-1941), who campaigned against the Ku Klux Klan and for the Scottsboro Boys.

Mr Underwood drinks cherry wine in his office; he is named after Braxton Bragg, a Confederate general (Atticus says this practice makes the child so named into a slow drinker) who was outspoken, indecisive, and before the Civil War, an owner of slaves himself.

Zeebo

We encounter him as the rubbish collector who has to dispose of the dead dog, Tim Johnson, and disinfect the area outside the Radleys' house in Chapter 10.

Then, in Chapter 12, we see him in a completely different light, as he leads the hymns at Calpurnia's church. He is in fact her son, which is why he can read. He has children himself. Calpurnia is, therefore, a grandmother; we can take it that her grandchildren are better people than Alexandra's grandson Francis Hawkins (see Chapter 9).

Mr Horace Gilmer

The circuit solicitor who prosecutes Tom Robinson; Atticus' opponent in court. He comes from Abbottsville. He is balding, smooth-faced; aged anywhere between 40 and 60 (the book doesn't tell us). He has a squint.

His various unpleasant features extend to the complacent and arrogant way in which he questions Tom in court. Tom's admission that he helped Mayella Ewell *because he felt sorry for her* breaks a cultural taboo. Gilmer exploits this.

He knows that he does not have to put a proper case in court, because Tom will be found guilty as charged regardless of the evidence. This would be different if the judge had the power to pass the verdict; but it is in the hands of the jury, not Judge Taylor.

Reverend Sykes

Introduced in Chapter 12- he is a community leader, where morality is concerned, just as Atticus is. But Atticus' "congregation"- the adults of Maycomb in general, and the jury at the trial in particular- does not listen to him, when he calls on them to do what is right.

Rev Sykes is a short, stocky man, who stands, in his church, in a black suit and black tie, with a white shirt, and a gold watch chain (like Atticus)- Chapter 12. His eyes are black (Chapter 17).

He is kind to Jem and Scout, and respectful and appreciative of Atticus' efforts on Tom's behalf.

The Haverfords

In Chapter 1, Atticus' first two clients were members of this family, who killed a local blacksmith in an argument over a horse. They refused to plead guilty, and so were hanged. The family's stupidity means that they have a reputation for being jackasses.

Miss Rachel Haverford, Dill's aunt and Atticus' neighbour, is allegedly an alcoholic who drinks whisky for breakfast. Her character is not developed; she is needed simply to make a fuss when she disapproves of what Dill does.

She is a social traditionalist. She disapproves of Atticus' agreeing to defend Tom Robinson, and says that, in doing so, he was choosing to bang his head against a wall, because the effort would be futile and wasted (Chapter 22).

Francis Hancock

He is Aunt Alexandra's grandson. He is one year older than Scout (he is eight); he slicks his hair back and asks for dull Christmas presents, and is the "most boring child" Scout has ever met. He tells tales. He lives in Mobile.

He describes Dill as "a little runt" and a stray dog. He is a thoroughly unpleasant child, who reflects badly on Alexandra, and serves to show how easily, and how young, children will pick up racist attitudes from the adults around them.

Cousin Ike Finch

Maycomb County's last surviving Confederate veteran. He mentions the Missouri Compromise (see index of historical terms).

Mrs Henry Lafayette Dubose

She lives two doors to the north of the Finch family.

Her characterisation is negative, in every way; she was "plain hell", and vicious to the children. Everyone considers her "the meanest old woman who ever lived".

She features for the first time in Chapter 11. We discover that she is very old; almost bedridden; and rumoured to have a CSA pistol - a Confederate Army relic. She always looks angry, and she always criticises and insults the children; "we could do nothing to please her".

She has a Negro servant, a girl called Jessie.

She is a terrifying, prejudiced and racist, witch-like woman. She has died by the end of Chapter 12. It is only then that we find that she was suffering with the pain from terminal cancer. She is in the novel as a means of showing Jem and Scout that courage is not firing a gun at a defenceless dog; it is taking on a fight you cannot win, and doing what you can to retain your own self-control and your own integrity.

Miss Caroline Fisher

She is Scout's teacher in her first term. She is aged 21 or less, with pink cheeks, red nail-polish, and bright auburn hair.

She wears a red and white striped dress; she looks and smells like a peppermint drop. She comes from Winston County, North Alabama. Scout thinks that she is probably a Republican, and anti-prohibition. Scout says she is a pretty little thing.

She lodges in Miss Maudie Atkinson's upstairs front room.

Rather like Aunt Alexandra, she is a figure of ridicule, because her theories and approach to educating young children are completely wrong-headed.

Helen Robinson

She is mentioned in chapter 12- she collapses in chapter 25, when Atticus tells her that her husband Tom has been killed.

Mr Link Deas

He is mentioned in Chapter 11. He is a cotton farmer, and he has a shop. He has employed Tom all year round for eight years and has found him entirely reliable.

He is one of the group of men who call on Atticus in Chapter 15, anticipating that a mob will try to snatch (and murder) Tom the night before his trial.

He is ejected from the court after he intervenes as a character witness for Tom, in Chapter 19.

He employs Tom's widow Helen (Chapter 27), not because he needs her to work for him, but because he wants to do something to redress the wrongs done to Tom. When Bob Ewell harasses Helen, he confronts and threatens Ewell

He is in the novel as a character who, like Atticus and Miss Maudie, does not discriminate on the grounds of race. Maycomb needs a few of these people to counteract the Ewells and Duboses.

Eula May

She neither speaks nor appears, but she is Maycomb's telephone operator. She telephones to give residents public information- school closures, wedding invitations, and first aid advice when the doctor is out of town. In an earlier, pre-mobile phone age, she is the human equivalent of unlimited texts.

Calpurnia asks her to alert everyone who has a phone that there is a mad dog on the street (Chapter 10).

Dr Reynolds

He attends to the dying old Mr Radley; and to Jem's broken arm. Like Atticus, he accepts payment in kind for his services, such as a bushel of potatoes for delivering a baby.

Chuck Little

He "didn't know where his next meal was coming from, but a born gentleman". He despises the Ewells. His real name is Charles.

Mr (Dick) Avery

He boards (rents a room) across the street from Mrs Dubose. He sits on the porch sneezing till 9 pm. He takes money out of the church collection. He has a big stomach; he is almost stuck in an upstairs window when he, and all the other men, help to salvage Miss Maudie's belongings from her burning house.

He is the subject Jem turns into a snowman, in Chapter 8. He blames the children for bringing the snow, by behaving badly.

Miss Sarah Barber and Miss Frances Barber

Introduced as late as Chapter 27, they are two unmarried sisters, said to be Republicans, who moved from Clanton, Alabama in 1911 and live in a house where they built a cellar. Known as Tutti and Frutti, they are both deaf. At Hallowe'en the previous year, children (including Scout) played a trick on them, hiding their furniture in the cellar.

These characters are in the novel to explain why there is a formal Hallowe'en pageant at the school- necessitating the walk in the dark which enables Bob Ewell to attack Jem and Scout.

Index of historical and geographical references

Chapter 1

General Andrew Jackson (1767-1843). A lawyer and general. He was elected as US President (1829-1837) as a champion of individual freedom.

The Creeks- a tribe of American Indians, native to Alabama and Georgia.

Methodists- the dominant religious denomination in Alabama; Methodism spread rapidly from 1739 onwards, and the Methodist Church separated from the Church of England in 1791.

Mobile the third largest city in Alabama, with a population of approx. 200,000 today

Saint Stephens Now abandoned; it served as the capital of the (eastern) Alabama territory, from 1817-19.

John Wesley (1703-91) founder of the Methodist church, in England; he planned to export Methodism to America from 1760. He believed that when Christians allowed the love of God to be "supreme in their hearts", they achieve a state of holiness. There is an argument that this is where Atticus' superiority as a human being comes from. The Ladies' Missionary Society in Maycomb is part of the Methodist Episcopal Church South, which split from its parent church in 1845 because of its belief that slavery was legitimate.

The Maycomb ladies belong to a church which is almost wholly white, because freed slaves had left to join the other arm of the Methodists. It supported prohibition and slavery.

Montgomery   the capital of Alabama; Atticus trained as a lawyer there. In 1956, the Afro-American population boycotted the buses, forcing the breakdown of segregation and the start of the civil rights movement in America.

Code of Alabama Dated 1901, it enforced racial segregation in schools, and restated the illegality of inter-racial marriage.

Hoover carts – car bodies converted into carts drawn by mules.

Meridian, Mississippi A city with a population today of about 40,000. It was an important hub for rail transport and it was the largest city in Mississippi from 1890 to 1930.

Dracula- film based on Bram Stoker's novel, and issued in 1931 by Universal Studios, starring Bela Lugosi**.**

Oliver Optic- the pseudonym of William T Adams (1822-97), a schoolteacher, who wrote boys' adventure novels.

Victor Appleton - a pseudonym or house name under which a group of ghost writers published the tales of Tom Swift (1910-1941). These were adventure novels featuring inventions and science fiction. The acronym TASER comes from "Thomas A Swift's Electric Rifle".

Edgar Rice Burroughs- American author (1875-1950) of the Tarzan stories.

The Rover Boys- a series of 30 boys' adventure books published between 1899 and 1926, and written by Edward Stratemeyer under the pseudonym Arthur M Winfield. He was also involved in the Tom Swift series.

Tom Swift- see above, under Victor Appleton

Old Sarum- this is where the Cunninghams live. There is also a place called Old Sarum in Wiltshire, near Salisbury and Stonehenge. At that site, there are the remains of a 400BC hill fort, and indications of habitation as far back as 3000 BC. Is Harper Lee using the name to imply that the Cunninghams and the other rural farmers are in fact cavemen with prehistoric attitudes?

Auburn - a city in eastern Alabama with a population today of 60000. It has a university and highly regarded schools.

Tuscaloosa a city of about 100000 people; the fifth largest in Alabama. It has a large hospital and is a centre or the care of people with mental health issues.

Pensacola - a city in western Florida.

The Grey Ghost – see the entry under chapter 31.

Chapter 2

Tarzan and the Ant Men- first published in 1924-the tenth of Edgar Rice Burroughs' Tarzan books

Winston County, North Alabama- formerly known as Hancock County until 1858; a county in Alabama,with a population of about 25000.

Alabama seceded from the Union on 11/1/1861.
By a vote of 61-39, Alabama declared itself a sovereign and independent state and left the United States- becoming the fourth state to do so. Delegates from five other states came to Montgomery a month later to set up the Confederate Congress or government. The secession document provided for trial by "impartial jury"- not at all what the State of Alabama gives Tom Robinson. It also prohibited the freedom of slaves.

Liquor Interests   supporters of the ending of prohibition and the legalised sale of alcohol.

Big Mules   Industrialists who want to see political power in Alabama reformed, to reflect the change from a farming to an industrial economy.

Lorenzo Dow diaries- Dow (1777-1834) was a Methodist preacher in the USA, Ireland and England. Much of his writing was published in one edition in 1854 and at one time it was outsold in America only by the Bible.

John Dewey (1859-1952) US educator, who opposed authoritarian teaching methods, and advocated learning through experience. Perhaps this explains the lack of structure in Scout's class in Chapter 2, and the general waving about of flash cards. Dewey's theories played down the importance of learning from textbooks and by repetition.

Dewey Decimal System- a system of library classification invented by Melvil Dewey (1851-1931) in 1876. It is taught in American schools in grade 3 and upwards- which explains why Jem knows about it.

WPA jobs - construction jobs (building roads, schools, parks etc) set up under FD Roosevelt's "New Deal" and the Works Progress Administration, to counter the Great Depression. It started in 1935; over 8 years, it provided almost 8 million jobs. It aimed to provide work for the breadwinner of each family where the breadwinner was a long-time unemployed citizen, and certified as being in need.

(what the) Sam Hill- a euphemism for "what the hell?" It originated in the 1830s. Sam Hill was a shopkeeper in Arizona whose store supplied many strange and wonderful items! There were also other historical figures called Sam Hill, to whom the expression may refer.

Chapter 4

L & N Railroad The Louisville and Nashville railroad operated almost 8000 miles of track in 13 states by 1925; it included a line from Montgomery and Mobile to New Orleans

Good Citizenship- a concept mentioned by President Theodore Roosevelt in a speech in 1902.

Chapter 5

Second Battle of the Marne-18/7/1918-6/8/1918- the Allies checked the final German offensive in World War 1 in a major battle.

Brigadier Joe Wheeler (1836-1906) was a cavalry general for the Confederates in the Civil War (reporting to General Braxton Bragg), then a general in the US Army in the Spanish-American War, and a senator for Alabama from 1884 to 1900. His nickname was "fighting Joe". The idea of the daughters' bedrooms and their staircase at Finch Landing may be a reference to Wheeler's own house.

Chapter 8

Rosetta Stone- a large stone with hieroglyphics on it; found in 1799 in Egypt; now in the British Museum.

Appomattox- a village in Virginia where the Confederate Army surrendered on 9/4/1865, ending the American Civil War.

Chapter 9

General Hood- John Bell Hood (1831-1879). He lost his right leg and the use of his left arm as a result of war injuries. He died of yellow fever in New Orleans.

Missouri Compromise- an agreement in 1820-1, which divided the Louisiana Purchase area into a slave area in the south and a free area in the north. The Louisiana Purchase was 828,000 square miles of the western Mississippi valley, which America bought from France in 1802 for $15 million.

Stonewall Jackson (1824-63). Thomas Jonathan "Stonewall" Jackson was a successful Confederate general; he died after being shot, accidentally, by troops on his own side. His nicknames included "Old Blue Light". The hymn sung at Calpurnia's church (chapter 12) is very similar to Jackson's last words- "Let us cross over the river, and rest under the shade of the trees".

Mobile see entry under Chapter 1.

Lord Melbourne (1779-1848). Adviser to the young Queen Victoria; Prime Minister from 1835-41.

Chapter 10

Jew's Harp- an Alabama term for a type of harmonica played with the forefinger.

Chapter 11

Confederate Army relic a gun left over from the Civil War of 1861-5

CSA pistol – a gun manufactured for and issued by the Confederate States Army

Dixie Howell- Millard Fleming Howell (1912-1971), an American football and baseball player and coach. He played for the University of Alabama from 1932-4, then for the Washington Redskins.

Ivanhoe- an adventure/romance novel, published in 1820, by Sir Walter Scott; it deals with the difficulty of creating an integrated society in which both the Normans and the Saxons can live; rather like the issues of segregation and social cohesion in Alabama! Film versions were made in America in 1911 and 1913.

Chapter 12

Sit down strikes in Birmingham- the most famous of these was on **Christmas Eve 1936,** when black steel workers downed tools at the American Casting Company; they secured a 20% pay rise and overtime pay.

Bread lines- queues of unemployed and often homeless men who were fed by charities and churches

Mardi Gras- Shrove Tuesday, celebrated in New Orleans; a Catholic celebration.

Hunt's The Light of the World- William Holman Hunt painted this from 1851-3. It depicts Christ knocking at a door which has no handle, and can only be opened from the inside. The door represents "the obstinately shut mind". Having a copy of this painting in the First Purchase Church symbolises the struggle against the prejudice, or obstinately shut mind, of white superiority- just as, for Atticus, defending Tom is as much a "lost cause" as the Civil War became to the Southern states.

Impurity of Women doctrine a strand of doctrine in the Catholic and other churches, which uses the Bible to try to justify the refusal to ordinate women priests, and the story of Adam and Eve to denigrate women in comparison with men.

Blackstone's Commentaries- Sir William Blackstone (1723-1780); his "Commentaries on the Laws of England" (1765-9) influenced the American legal system greatly.

Chapter 13

Shinny- illegal, or "moonshine", alcohol

Tight - tipsy/drunk

Rice Christians- a term, first used in Asia, to denote someone who embraces Christianity because doing so brings material benefits, rather than out of genuine religious belief.

Governor William Wyatt Bibb (1781-1820) was a US senator and the first Governor of Alabama.

Reconstruction- the period from 1865-1877 when the southern states were occupied by US federal government troops.

Chapter 15

Henry Woodfin Grady (1850-1889) was a journalist and newspaper owner; he called for a "new South" with investment in new technology, new prosperity, but with a continuing emphasis on white supremacy.

Ku Klux Klan- a society founded in 1866 to maintain white supremacy. It re-emerged in 1915 and was popular in the 1920s.

Southern womanhood- a convention that white women were to be treated deferentially, admired and protected. The genteel white woman would live a pious and pure life, and cultivate and shape the moral values within their own family. The abolition of slavery implied that the status of white women in the South would be lowered; this promoted the concept of the white supremacist movement and the Ku Klux Klan. It saw protecting white womanhood as part of its mission, and it attracted members of white upper-class families as a result.

"Nearer my God to thee"- a hymn written in 1841 by Sarah Flower Adams; it is included in the Methodist hymn book of 1933. It was also played by the band of the defeated Confederate Army at the Battle of Gettysburg. Atticus sings it. It is about the ladder which connects the redeemed soul with God. Atticus is a morally superior and godly human being, so it is a suitable theme tune for him; it is also associated with consolation in times of disaster- such as the miscarriage of justice in chapter 21- and the sinking of the "Titanic"!.

Chapter 16

Mennonites- an extreme Protestant sect; they still emerge from the back woods for the trial of Tom Robinson.

William Jennings Bryan 1860-1925- a lawyer, politician and orator who stood for the US presidency three times.

Courthouse burnt in 1856 The state of Alabama has several court houses modelled on the architecture of Greek temples- such as the Wilcox County courthouse of 1858.

Braxton Bragg (1817-1876) a sometimes unpopular Confederate general, he married into a rich family and became a slave-owning owner of a sugar plantation. He is buried in Mobile, Alabama.

Chapter 17

Robert E Lee (1807-70) The overall commander of the Confederate Army during the American Civil War. Bob Ewell is (fatuously) named after him.

Chapter 20

Thomas Jefferson (1743-1826) Third president of the USA; he helped to draft the Declaration of Independence, which Atticus is referring to, for its doctrine of legal fairness and equality.

Rockefellers JD Rockefeller (1839-1937) owned almost all of the oil refineries in the USA. He was so wealthy that he could afford to set up a medical research institute with $500m in 1901, and to help many other good causes.

Chapter 23

Chester County - part of the state of Pennsylvania.

Enfield Prison Farm - a correctional institute in Connecticut known until July 1960 as Osborn Prison Farm.

Chapter 24

Mrunas A fictional tribe in Africa.

J Grimes Everitt   A fictional missionary, sponsored by the white church in Maycomb to convert African tribes to Christianity.

Mrs Roosevelt in Birmingham   Eleanor Roosevelt (1884-1962) was married to the President FD Roosevelt. She joined the NAACP (National Association for the Advancement of Colored People). In the auditorium in Birmingham, Alabama, where the Southern Conference on Human Welfare held its first meeting, she refused to comply with segregated seating and sat in the aisle. Interestingly, this was in 1938- after the time in which the novel is set!!

Chapter 26

Elmer Davis (1890-1958) A journalist and broadcaster; twelve million people would listen to his nightly five-minute newscasts by 1941. He then became the head of the US Office of War Information.

Chapter 27

WPA- the Works Progress Administration scheme which created jobs for 8 million people during the Great Depression.

Bob Taylor- Robert Love Taylor (1850-1912) was governor of Tennessee and a US senator.

Ladies' Law- included in the Alabama Code of 1901, it makes swearing within the hearing of any girl or woman a criminal offence.

Cotton Tom Heflin- a Republican congressman and senator, who was Secretary of State in Alabama at the start of the 20th century.

NRA- we do our part- the slogan of the **National Recovery Administration**. The US Supreme Court found it unconstitutional in 1935. Hence the comment that the National Recovery Act was dead.

Clanton, Alabama- the main town in Chilton County, Alabama. Its population is less than 10000 people.

New Orleans A city in Louisiana; its population today is about 350000. The home of the Mardi Gras. It was to become a central city in the civil rights struggle of the 1960s.

Ad astra per aspera- a saying in Latin, which translates as "**to the stars, through harsh times**"-not "from the mud to the stars", as Mrs Merriweather claims. Both translations, though, have something to say about the distance Maycomb has to travel before it can claim to be enlightened!

Chapter 28

Haints- a colloquial dialect term for a ghost or apparition or lost soul (the same as "haunt").

Spanish-American War- a short conflict over control of Cuba, in 1898.

Colonel Maycomb- an imaginary figure, as Maycomb is a made-up place. Interestingly, there is a Macomb County in Michigan, named after a military veteran, Colonel Alexander Macomb (1782-1841).

Creek Indian Wars- in 1813-14; a small war which ended with the Creek Indians surrendering to Andrew Jackson and giving up half of Alabama and part of southern Georgia to the government of the United States.

Chapter 31

The Grey Ghost - one of the eleven popular novels by Robert F Schulkers, published between 1921 and 1932.

The Film Version of the Novel
– and what it can add to your understanding

The film version, made in 1962, runs for 129 minutes and is readily available on DVD (try Amazon). Gregory Peck won an Oscar for his portrayal of Atticus. The acting of the three children's parts is very strong too.

Aunt Alexandra does not appear at all in the film; Mrs Dubose only for a minute or so; Calpurnia's role, and Miss Maudie's, are minimal, and Dill's Aunt becomes Stephanie (Crawford) instead of Rachel Haverford. Judge Taylor's character is played down, and the (minor) parts of Horace Gilmer and Dr Reynolds are played by actors who do not resemble their descriptions in the novel; neither does Heck Tate.

This extensive editing is necessary, to reduce the novel to an acceptable length on screen. All of the religious material- we find it in chapters 12 and 24- is left out. So are all of the classroom scenes, including the scene with Miss Gates "teaching" Scout's class about Hitler and democracy. There is no sight, in the film, of the Ewells' shack, and the Ewells, and their fellow farmers' children, do not appear as scruffy or dirty as we might expect. The film seems uninterested in projecting a "white trash" underclass; perhaps it is uncomfortable to acknowledge that it even exists.

The humour of the playing out of the Boo Radley game is missing. Because Miss Maudie has only a very small role (as an emergency babysitter), the burning down of her house, and the snow, is nowhere to be seen. The Christmas scenes are missing, and, with them, the direct accusations of "nigger-loving", which we find only in the mouth of Bob Ewell, and not current among the children (Cecil Jacobs and Francis Hancock do not appear).

These editorial decisions are made mainly because the timescale of the novel needs to be concentrated, in the film, to make the action more continuous and less episodic. We are left with the children's fascination with the Radley place; the shooting of Tim Johnson, the mad dog, which leaves Jem with an unspoken admiration for Atticus; and with three main episodes- the trial itself (chapters 17-21); the attack by Bob Ewell, and Boo's rescue, as Scout and Jem walk home (Chapters 28-31); and the scene where the lynch mob demands that Atticus hands Tom Robinson to them (from Chapter 15).

The motif of killing a mockingbird appears twice. The second occasion is at the end of the film, where Scout's words are used. The earlier one is from Chapter 10, but the setting is switched to Walter Cunningham's lunch visit, and Atticus says that his own father told him about the "sin" of shooting this type of songbird- in the novel, it is Atticus' own idea.

In the novel, we do not see Ewell spit at Atticus. We read a report of the incident, as related by Miss Stephanie Crawford, who says it took place at the post office (Chapter 23), and Tom's shooting is reported in chapter 24. In the film, the spitting takes place outside the Robinsons' house (where Tom's father is a new character). Atticus has gone there to inform Helen that Tom has been killed already, trying to escape on the journey from the courthouse to prison by car.

At the end of the trial, Judge Taylor dismisses the jury in the film, and goes into his room, slamming the door- a clear sign that he sees the "guilty" verdict as wrong and may set it aside. The film uses only the end of Chapter 21, but not what precedes it- because the impressionistic writing in that chapter would be difficult to capture on film.

The lynch mob scene is very effective and menacing, and it shows Jem and Scout rescuing Atticus and defusing the tension in a powerful way. The character of Mr Underwood is left out- Atticus has no protection in the film as he does in the book, from his shotgun.

The film version is faithful to the parts of the novel it uses, and it captures much of its character, by using specific pieces of dialogue, and by presenting the Radleys as unseen, unspeaking people who can easily be imagined to be fiends.

It is less true to the spirit of the novel in its presentation of racism, and of the incestuous relationship Ewell has with his oldest daughter. We should remember that many of the cinema-going public in America in 1962 and the years after it had still to be convinced that racial segregation was morally and fundamentally wrong. The miscarriage of justice is presented as being due mainly to Tom's one-handedness and Ewell's left-handedness- it is the result of a wilful misreading of the evidence, not a determined, vicious racial prejudice.

Atticus shows why Tom is innocent, and he explains Mayella's motivation- that, having made the socially unspeakable error of "tempting a Negro", her guilt and shame led her to want to get rid of him completely, regardless of the truth, or of the consequences for him.

If the film had been made ten or twenty years later, the reasons for the jury's bias and prejudice- its inherent racism- could and would have been dealt with more frankly and explicitly. It is interesting that the Ewells are not depicted as the "trash" they are in the novel.

In the film, we see Calpurnia very much as a servant, and not so much as the surrogate mother she is in the novel. The absence of the character of Alexandra makes this inevitable. The film has no time for, or no interest in, Dolphus Raymond's interracial liberalism, or the children's several discussions of the common, shared origins of all people of all races in the mists of time.

In this sense, the film is a product of its own time, and less forward-looking or principled than the novel. The film version is less about the evil of racism and segregation, and Atticus as the man the community trusts, respects, and expects to do its unwanted jobs; and more about Atticus as the conscientious widower and single parent, and his personal warmth and wisdom. In the film version, the drama is rooted, in the end, in the family life of the Finches, rather than in the shortcomings of small town America, and, by extension, all of America.

It isn't the fault of the film that it is a film. It is a different art form, and it needs a narrative to sustain it. It needs to be visual. It has less time than the novel to be reflective, or symbolic. Judged as a film, it is very well done, moving, and a sensitive representation of parts of the novel on which it is "based".

If you watch it- and there is no harm in seeing it, because it will reinforce your admiration for the book- remember two things; first, that it is not trying to be a film version of the novel (unlike a film version of a stage play); and, secondly, that, with the passing of another fifty years, since 1962, our definitions of the immorality of racism and prejudice have moved on from what was accepted- or could be discussed widely in the cinema- at the time the film was made.

Another way of putting that point is this. Imagine you were reinterpreting the novel, in a feature film, today. Would you make childhood look like this? Parents like this? A film like this?

I doubt you would. The issues today are not about growing up annoying the neighbours and playing in the street; they are about different dangers and different experiences, because you are growing up in a different kind of society.

Final Tips for success

A few pages back, in the example essays, you'll have seen that what counts is organising what you want to say (your plan!), then working steadily and succinctly through it. What would be even better of course … would be to know in the first place what question you are going to get! Sadly, there is no answer to that.

And yet…questions do come in set styles. It may surprise you, but examiners go to great pains to choose questions that candidates **will** be able to answer well!

Whatever your exam board is, look on its website, not just at questions on past papers, but at the mark schemes and the examiners' reports. Ask your English teacher to demystify the mark scheme and give you some tips.

And a pitfall to avoid

Don't fall into the trap of having a list of quotations you're determined to force into any essay. If you know the book- which you surely must by now!!- suitable short references will pop into your head (a two or three word quotation, for example, "Maycomb's usual disease" as a way of describing how Atticus refers to his town's dreadful, casual racism).

Your number one focus is on answering the question in front of you.

Your number two focus is on answering the question.

So is focus number 3.

Answering the question means taking it apart and highlighting the key words (often that little word "how"); making a proper plan, which organises your material, gives you an argument and leads you to a clear and convincing conclusion; writing your essay from the plan; and stopping when you get to the end.

A proper plan means an essay that needs nothing added after its conclusion.

Please, please resist the temptation to start writing your essay straight away, even if many of those around you in the exam room do just that.

Raise your grade tip:

Check-constantly- that what you are writing is actually answering the question in front of you. If it isn't- leave it out.

Especially if you are taking your GCSE this summer, I wish you every success.

Gavin Smithers is a private tutor, covering Broadway, Chipping Campden and the North Cotswolds. He has an English degree from Oxford University, and a passion for helping others to discover the joy and satisfaction of great literature.

Gavin's Guides are short books packed with insight. Their key aim is to help you raise your grade!

The series is available as e-book and paperback. Details and reviews of the series are on Gavin Smithers' Amazon page.

Titles include:

> *Understanding J.B. Priestley's An Inspector Calls*
> *Understanding William Golding's Lord of the Flies*
> *Understanding Charles Dickens' Great Expectations*
> *Understanding John Steinbeck's Of Mice and Men*
> *Understanding Emily Dickinson's Set Poems*
> *Understanding Edward Thomas' Set Poems*

And finally………if there's anything you're still not sure about, and if your teacher can't help, please contact the author-
grnsmithers@hotmail.co.uk

21868625R00100

Made in the USA
San Bernardino, CA
09 June 2015